●●● **Julie Moore**

Common mistakes at

Proficiency

... and how to avoid them

CAMBRIDGE
UNIVERSITY PRESS

University Printing House, Cambridge CB2 8BS, United Kingdom

One Liberty Plaza, 20th Floor, New York, NY 10006, USA

477 Williamstown Road, Port Melbourne, VIC 3207, Australia

314–321, 3rd Floor, Plot 3, Splendor Forum, Jasola District Centre, New Delhi – 110025, India

103 Penang Road, #05-06/07, Visioncrest Commercial, Singapore 238467

Cambridge University Press is part of the University of Cambridge.

It furthers the University's mission by disseminating knowledge in the pursuit of education, learning and research at the highest international levels of excellence.

www.cambridge.org
Information on this title: www.cambridge.org/9780521606837

© Cambridge University Press 2005

First published 2005

20 19 18 17 16 15 14 13 12 11 10

Printed in Great Britain by CPI Group (UK) Ltd, Croydon CR0 4YY

A catalogue record for this publication is available from the British Library

ISBN 978-0-521-60683-7 Paperback

Designed and produced by Kamae Design, Oxford

Contents

1 Will or would?

1 Tick the correct sentence in each pair.

1 a Everything will be much quicker when we will get the new computer system.
  b Everything will be much quicker when we get the new computer system.
2 a I promised Mum I'd go straight home after the concert.
  b I promised Mum I'll go straight home after the concert.

We use *will* to talk about future possibilities or predictions which we believe will happen, especially based on an existing situation or evidence:
If you don't water the plants, they'll die. (it's a certain fact)
My journey to work will be much easier when the new tram line opens. (the line is already being built, so the consequences are quite certain)
☆ We only use *will* to talk about the possibility or prediction, not in the *if / when* clause. (not ~~when the new tram line will open~~)

We use *would* to describe hypothetical possibilities which are uncertain, unlikely or impossible, often based on situations which do not yet exist or can never exist:
I'd buy more organic products if they weren't so expensive. (but they <u>are</u> expensive)
In my opinion, it would be disastrous to let this project go ahead. (no decision has been made yet, so the consequences are only a possibility)

We also use *would* to talk about a time in the future from a point in the past:
They planned that they would meet at midnight.

2 Correct the mistake below.

You .... the heating.

You told me last week that you will come and fix the heating, but it's still freezing in here!

3 Underline the correct form to complete each sentence.

1 It *will be / would be* nice to go away for longer, but I can't get more time off work.
2 She told me she *will call / would call* if there was a problem.
3 If this rain *continues / will continue* much longer, the river will flood.
4 Based on current estimates, the number of mobile phone users *will double / would double* in the next five years.
5 Dave *will be / would be* furious if he knew what you'd done.
6 If everything *goes / will go* to plan, we'll have everything finished by Friday.
7 He promised he *will be / would be* back in time for my birthday.
8 More people would use public transport if the services *were / would be* more reliable.

2 Which modal do I use?

1 Tick the correct sentence in each pair.

1 a   If you like Impressionist art, you should visit the Musée d'Orsay in Paris.
  b   If you like Impressionist art, you have to visit the Musée d'Orsay in Paris.
2 a   I think that children should respect their parents.
  b   I think that children must respect their parents.

We use *should* to talk about what we think is right, best or correct:
*I don't think people **should** keep big dogs in small apartments.*

We use *have to* to talk about what is necessary or compulsory:
*Do young men **have to** do military service in your country?*

We also use *must* to talk about what is necessary or compulsory, especially when the subject of the verb is not a person or when the main verb is passive:
*All applications **must** be received by 31 January.*

☆ In the negative, *mustn't* means 'not allowed', but *don't have to* means 'not necessary':
*The cheque **must not** exceed the value of the guarantee card.*
*EU citizens **don't have to** get a visa to travel to the US.*

We use *must* to talk about what we are sure is true. The opposite is *can't*:
*She **must** be bored at home all day on her own.*
*You **can't** be tired – you've only just got up!*

2 Correct the mistake below.

LUGGAGE SHOULD NOT
BE LEFT UNATTENDED
UNATTENDED LUGGAGE WILL BE
REMOVED AND MAY BE DESTROYED

Luggage .... unattended.

3 Complete the following sentences using an appropriate modal verb.

1 All children under 12 .... be accompanied by an adult.
2 There's a free 30-day trial period, so you .... pay anything for the first month.
3 I missed the last train and .... get a taxi home.
4 We .... need more sugar already – I only bought some last week.
5 All accidents .... be recorded in the incident book.
6 Have you seen their house? They .... have a lot of money.
7 That cut looks really bad – I think you .... go to hospital.
8 You .... lift the lid while the rice is cooking or all the steam will be released and it won't cook properly.

Which nouns and adjectives are followed by a gerund or an infinitive?

1 Tick the correct sentence in each pair.

1 a As a disabled person, he has difficulty getting on and off buses.
  b As a disabled person, he has difficulty to get on and off buses.

2 a I'm used to eating my main meal at midday.
  b I'm used to eat my main meal at midday.

Many words are followed by a verb in either the gerund *(-ing)* or infinitive *(to do)* form. You can check which patterns a word is used with by looking at the examples in a good learner's dictionary. The following are some common combinations:

- noun + *to do (something)*
  have the ability / confidence / courage to do (something):
  *He didn't have the **confidence to speak up** about what he'd witnessed.*
- noun (+ preposition) + gerund
  fear of doing (something), have difficulty in doing (something):
  *He lived in constant **fear of being found out**.*
- adjective + *to do (something)*
  be right / wrong to do (something), be lucky / fortunate to do (something)
  be happy to do (something) (= willing to do something):
  ***I'm happy to pick Jamie up** if you're busy.*
- adjective + gerund
  be used to doing (something), be busy doing (something), be worth doing (something):
  *The vineyards **are well worth visiting**.*
☆ See Unit 29 for verb + verb combinations.

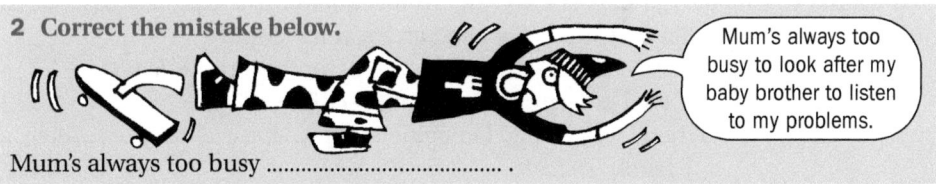

2 Correct the mistake below.

Mum's always too busy to look after my baby brother to listen to my problems.

Mum's always too busy ....

3 Use the words below (in the same order) to create sentences. Add any necessary prepositions or articles, and put the verbs in an appropriate form.

1 He / have / terrible / fear / travel / by / plane ....
2 She / be / right / tell / boss / about / problem ....
3 He / have / ability / play / highest / level / the / sport ....
4 We / have / difficulty / find / parking / space ....
5 It / be not / worth / cook / full / meal / for / one / person ....
6 I / feel / lucky / have / such / good / friends ....
7 He / not / have / courage / tell / her / face to face ....
8 He / be / not / used to / get up / so / early ....

1 Complete the text using *should*, *shouldn't* or *have to*.

Guidelines for travellers

Before you travel: You (1) .... check whether the country you are visiting has any visa requirements. To visit some countries you may (2) .... apply for a visa in advance. You (3) .... make sure that you have adequate travel insurance in case you need urgent medical treatment or, in extreme cases, (4) .... be flown home.

In the air: The atmosphere inside an aircraft can cause dehydration, so you (5) .... increase your fluid intake. You (6) .... , however, drink a lot of alcohol or caffeine. To avoid the effects of jet leg, you (7) .... try to sleep on the flight, especially if it's an eastbound journey. If you (8) .... take regular medication, you (9) .... take your normal dosage according to 'home time'.

2 Complete the sentences using the verb in brackets.

Example:

Yesterday:	'So, I'll see you outside the cinema at 8 o'clock tomorrow evening.'
Now:	We arranged that we *would meet outside the cinema* at 8. *(meet)*
1 January	'I'll give up smoking this year.'
Now:	At the start of the year, I resolved that I .... *(stop)*
2 Last night:	'I'll give you a call when I arrive at the airport.'
Now:	She said she .... at the airport. *(call)*
3 20 years ago:	'When I grow up, I'll have lots of children.'
Now:	When I was young, I imagined that .... a big family. *(have)*
4 January:	'The building work should be finished by the end of March.'
April:	We thought that the building work .... by now. *(finish)*
5 Last week:	'Don't worry, I'll bring some sleeping bags.'
Now:	'Where are the sleeping bags? You said you .... them.' *(bring)*
6 1950s:	'In 50 years' time, people will be living on the moon.'
Now:	Experts predicted that people .... on the moon by now. *(live)*
7 Tuesday:	'We'll probably be back in a couple of days.'
Sunday:	We didn't think the trip .... this long. *(take)*

3 Underline the most appropriate form of the verb to complete the horoscope.

Aries: 21 March – 19 April

The planet Mars is moving into your sign this week giving you the confidence (1) *to push / of pushing* ahead with career plans. If you've been hoping for a promotion at work, the next few days (2) *would bring / will bring* good news. For those of you disillusioned with your job, now is the time when you (3) *must / should* consider looking for something new – you have the ability (4) *to go / of going* right to the top and you don't (5) *have to / must* put up with second best. If your current boss is too busy (6) *to worry / worrying* about his own position to notice your achievements, you (7) *should / would* be looking for an organisation where you can realise your full potential. You might (8) *be / have to* wait a while for the right opportunity to make your move, but be patient; the wait (9) *will be / would be* well worth it!

4 Complete the sentences using the correct form of an appropriate verb.

Cricket star banned for six months

Cricketer John Wilson received a 6-month ban yesterday for failing to take a routine drugs test. The 36-year-old star says it was a simple mistake, but the authorities insist that all players must co-operate with random testing or face the consequences. What do you think? Have your say …

'I think he's lucky not (1) .... a longer ban. It isn't worth (2) .... a random drug testing program if players can just ignore the tests.'

'All sportsmen are role models for young people and they should take their responsibilities more seriously. Surely it (3) .... that difficult to remember to go for a simple test! The authorities are right (4) .... him as a warning to other top players that no one is above the rules.'

'I think a 6-month ban is too much. If he'd been found guilty (5) .... drugs, then that'd be different. But he just made a stupid mistake and I think it's wrong (6) .... him so harshly.'

'Drugs in sport is a serious problem and the sports authorities have to have the courage (7) .... the rules. If a top team are unlucky enough (8) .... one of their best players for a season, I think that's a price worth (9) ....'

5 The text below contains six errors. Find them and correct them.

Sweatshop labour is a problem in many countries. At one factory we visited, workers should work for 12 hours a day in a noisy, cramped workshop. The workers say nothing about conditions for fear to lose their jobs. Many families have difficulty to earn enough money to survive and many people are happy accepting jobs many miles from their homes. Valentina must travel 3 hours a day to get to work and back. She says that the government has to do something to improve conditions for workers like her, but she doesn't believe that things will change quickly.

4 Which, who or what?

1 Tick the correct sentence in each pair.

1 a The living room has a big open fire, which makes it really warm and cosy.
  b The living room has a big open fire, what makes it really warm and cosy.

2 a He has three brothers which are older than him.
  b He has three brothers who are older than him.

Who and *which* are used to refer back to something from the first part of a sentence. *Who* refers to people and *which* to things, places or organisations:
*Do you know **the guy who** lives next door?*
*I work for **an organisation which** helps homeless people find work.*

What is used to refer to something unknown:
*Do you know **what's** in the box?*

A defining relative clause defines exactly who or what you are talking about. *Who* or *which* can be replaced by *that* or sometimes dropped altogether:
*That's the man **who** I saw running away from the accident.*
*That's the man **(that)** I saw running away from the accident.*

A non-defining relative clause, separated by commas, gives extra information:
*Our apartment, **which** faces east, gets the sun in the morning.*

Which can't be dropped or replaced by *that*, as it would then become a defining relative clause, e.g. *Our house that faces east gets the sun in the morning.* (we have several houses and this one faces east)

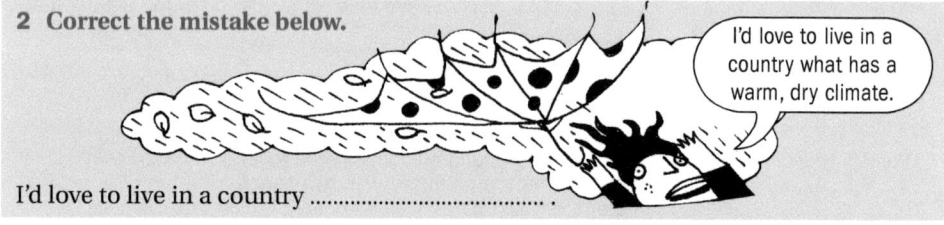

2 Correct the mistake below.

I'd love to live in a country what has a warm, dry climate.

I'd love to live in a country ....

3 Make the following sentences sound more natural using *who*, *which* or *what*.

Example: They have a very heavy workload. ~~A heavy workload~~ *which* can lead to stress.

1 There are many students. These students can't afford to pay such high fees.
2 We're lucky to live in this country. This country has free basic healthcare.
3 The book has two main characters. These characters are very different.
4 He hasn't explained the thing he wants me to do.
5 I stayed with a lovely family. This family live in an old farmhouse.
6 People are living longer. This means that the state has to pay more in pensions.
7 Do you know the thing he plans to do when he finishes college?
8 My uncle gave me some helpful advice about loans. My uncle is a bank manager.

Which pronoun do I use to refer to people in general?

1 **Tick the more natural sentence in each pair.**

1 a I think that you should stand up for what you believe in.
  b I think that one should stand up for what one believes in.

2 a If a student has a problem, he should see his personal tutor first.
  b If students have a problem, they should see their personal tutor first.

As English does not have a neutral third person singular pronoun, we have to find other ways of referring to an unknown or theoretical third person.

One can be used to refer to people in general. However, it is now becoming slightly old-fashioned and is normally used only in formal written contexts:
*Such difficulties are not surprising when **one** considers the size of the task at hand.*

We use *you* to refer to people in general or to any person in a hypothetical situation:
*If **you** want to succeed in business, **you** need confidence and determination.*

He used as a neutral pronoun is old-fashioned and considered sexist by some people. We sometimes use *they* as a neutral singular pronoun. Some people consider this incorrect in written English, but it is becoming more accepted and can be used in exams.
*What's the first thing you should say to **a customer** when **they** walk into the office?*

Other words used to describe people in general include *anyone, someone, people*:
*It's easy to understand how **anyone** would get frustrated in that situation.*
*If **someone** retires at the age of 60, **they** will receive a full state pension.*

2 Correct the mistake below.

But .... ?

3 **Complete the text using appropriate pronouns.**

Christmas can be difficult if you think of (1) .... as a friend to the environment.
No one wants to spend the festive season wringing (2) .... hands about all the
paper wasted on cards or unnecessary plastic toys. But there are ways that
(3) .... can enjoy it without denting (4) .... eco-friendly conscience.
If (5)................... look around, there are plenty of eco-presents to be found, especially
recycled ones. Anyone will be delighted to receive a diary which (6) .... know
was produced from recycled paper or a mouse mat made from old car tyres. Or for the
really green friend, (7) .... could always arrange to have a tree planted in
(8) .... name.

6 Which personal pronoun do I use?

1 Tick the correct sentence in each pair.

1 a We all really enjoyed ourself at the party.
   b We all really enjoyed ourselves at the party.
2 a Shall I book a table? How many people are we?
   b Shall I book a table? How many of us are there?

We use the reflexive pronoun *ourselves* to refer to a group of people we are part of:
*We'd be fooling **ourselves** if we said it was going to be an easy match.*

We use *yourself* to talk to one person and *yourselves* to address a group of people:
*Why don't you ask him **yourself**?* (when talking to one person)
*You should count **yourselves** lucky that no one was badly hurt.* (to several people)

We use *themselves* to refer to a group of people we are not part of:
*The children prepared everything **themselves**.*

We can also use *themselves* to refer to an unknown or theoretical person:
*What should you do if someone falls and hurts **themselves**?*
☆ See unit 5 on use of *they* for third person singular.

When we talk about the number of people in a group, we use *of us / them*:
*There are eight **of us**, so we'll have to go in two taxis.* (not ~~we are eight people~~)

2 Correct the mistake below.

You're here to represent your country and any players who get yourself into trouble will be sent straight home.

Any players who .... will be sent straight home.

3 Complete the sentences with an appropriate personal pronoun.

1 'There was a loud bang and everyone threw .... to the ground.'
2 We've done a good job and we can all be proud of ....
3 You should always warm up before exercise so that you don't injure
  ....
4 The boys found .... in a dangerous situation.
5 We couldn't play a proper match because there weren't enough of
  ....
6 Make sure you all leave .... enough time to get to the station.
7 You need to ask .... what's more important, your job or your family.
8 The government have left .... open to criticism.

TEST 2

1 Complete the comments below using *which, who* or *what*.

1 This is the couple .... owned the guesthouse where we stayed.

2 This is the beach .... we looked out onto.

3 Here's a picture of the little beach stall .... sold fried chicken.

4 And this is Sylvia .... ran the stall.

5 You saw these flowers everywhere. I don't know .... they were, but they were so lovely and colourful.

6 This is Nicolaos, ... was our guide when we went turtle-watching.

7 And this is the turtle we saw .... had come up onto the beach to lay eggs.

8 This is one of the local fishermen – I can't remember .... his name was.

2 Rewrite the sentences replacing the pronoun *one* with the word in brackets, making any other necessary changes.

1 One must play one's part in helping protect the environment. *(everyone)*

....

2 One should respect the local customs of the country one is visiting. *(tourists)*

....

3 If one promises to do something, one shouldn't go back on one's promise. *(you)*

....

4 When one enters a mosque, one is expected to remove one's shoes. *(someone)*

....

5 If one is found guilty of a crime, one has to accept the punishment. *(person)*

....

3 Complete the text with one of the pronouns from the box. Some are used more than once and some may not be used.

who	what	which	you
they	themselves	ourselves	yourself

I come from quite a large family. I've got two brothers and two sisters (1) .... are all older than me. People say that if (2) .... 're the youngest child, (3) .... get spoilt, but I don't agree. What (4) .... don't realise is that as the youngest, (5) .... always have a lot to live up to, and (6) .... 're always trying to be as good as your older siblings.

In my case, this was always going to be a tough task. My sister Sharon, (7) .... 's the oldest, went to medical school and is now a cardiac surgeon. My two brothers, Luke and Andrew, set (8) .... up in business a few years ago and now run a successful Internet advertising agency (9) .... has offices in London, Paris and New York. My other sister, (10) .... 's a talented linguist, works for the United Nations and travels all over the world.

As a child, family friends would always ask me (11) .... I wanted to do and I would shrug my shoulders. Thankfully, my parents have a great attitude. They always told us not to worry about what other people think and encouraged us just to be (12) .... They just want us all to be happy whatever we're doing.

4 There are eight mistakes in the text. Find and correct them.

I work for a charity what helps people which are homeless. Homeless people need more than a roof over his head. He may require support for mental health problems, addictions, lack of self-confidence or skills. We have developed a range of programmes who help homeless people to develop your self-confidence and skills and reintegrate into society. Our practical approach helps people to find safe, long-term accommodation and provides the support one needs to rebuild one's life.

5 Complete the sentences using the correct form of the verbs in the box.

enjoy yourself	find yourself	take care of yourself	be yourself
please yourself	lock yourself out	express yourself	

1 The boys climbed over a wall and .... in an apple orchard.
2 In the interview, you should just try to relax and ....
3 The children are encouraged to .... through painting.
4 Hey, stop talking about work! We're on holiday and we're meant to be here to
....
5 The caretaker has a spare set of keys in case any of the students ....
6 Mum, will you stop worrying! Helen and I are old enough to .... now.
7 Dinner's at 8 o'clock, but there's nothing planned for the afternoon, so you can all
.... until then.

When do I use *the*?

1 Tick the correct sentence in each pair.

1 a I hope I didn't give him a wrong address.
  b I hope I didn't give him the wrong address.
2 a She's a kind of person who likes everything to be in a right place.
  b She's the kind of person who likes everything to be in the right place.

We use *the* to refer to things which there can only be one of:

- *the main / only*: *I'll meet you outside **the main** entrance to the station.*
- *the first / last / next*: *We need to get off at **the next** bus stop.*
- *the right / wrong*: *You have to be in **the right** mood for a party.*
- *the best / biggest*, etc.: *This could be **the most important** decision you ever make.*
- *in the future / long term / short term*: *I don't plan to change jobs **in the near future**.*

We use *the* in a number of common expressions:

- *at the age of*:
  *He left home **at the age of** 16 to find work abroad.*
- *be the kind / sort of person who*:
  *He's **the kind of person** who says what he thinks.*
  *It's **the sort of area** where you don't go out alone at night.*
- *have / get / give the impression that*:
  *I **had the impression** that she was worried about something.*

2 Correct the mistake below.

I sometimes really wish we didn't live on a top floor.

I sometimes really wish ....

3 Are these sentences right or wrong? Correct those which are wrong.

1 I don't want to do something that I'll regret in a future. ....
2 Quick fixes won't help the situation in the long term. ....
3 Most people retire at their age of 60 or 65. ....
4 We often get the impression that a world is getting smaller. ....
5 Every day Mehmet walks 45 minutes to school in a next village. ....
6 One of the rescue workers said it was worst accident he'd ever seen.

  ....
7 These are not the sort of tourists we want to attract. ....
8 The weather got the worse later in the week. ....

8 How do I use *quite*, *very* and *really*?

1 Tick the correct sentence in each pair.

1 a We had quite a busy week.

  b We had a quite busy week.

2 a It really is true that English people drink a lot of tea.

  b It is really true that English people drink a lot of tea.

The position of these adverbs of degree (*quite*, *very*, *really*, etc.) is important and can sometimes change the meaning of the sentence:

*   *be + quite / very / fairly*, etc. *+ adjective*:

    *The weather **was quite cold** when we arrived.*

    *The neighbourhood where he grew up **was quite wealthy**.*

    *The hotel we stayed in **was very expensive**.*

    ☆ Note: *be + really + adjective*: *really* means 'very'

                  really + be + adjective / noun: *really* means 'actually / in fact':

    *I found out later that Peter **had been really ill**.* (he was very ill)

    *I found out later that Peter **really had been ill**.* (it was true that he was ill)

*   *quite + a + adjective + noun*:

    *It was **quite a cold day** when we arrived.*

    But: *a + really / very / fairly*, etc. *+ adjective + noun*:

    *We stayed in **a very expensive hotel**.*

    ☆ We cannot use adverbs of degree with adjectives expressing something absolute:

    ~~She is **quite pregnant**.~~ (either she is pregnant or not)

2 Correct the mistake below.

Yes, ...

3 Put the words in the correct order to form a sentence.

1 quite / large / went / I / school / to / a ....

2 really / had / wonderful / We / a / holiday ....

3 very / family / to / My / important / are / me ....

4 really / Maybe / was / his / true / story ....

5 quite / software / The / to / easy / is / use ....

6 really / Everyone / on / hard / to / worked / time / finish ....

7 fairly / We / to / city / live / centre / close / the ....

8 quite / apartment / building / is / new / a / in / Their ....

16

9 Less or fewer?

1 Tick the correct sentence in each pair.

1 a An ageing population means that there are less working people.
  b An ageing population means that there are fewer working people.
2 a People now have less money to spend on luxury goods.
  b People now have fewer money to spend on luxury goods.

We use *less* before an uncountable noun:
*Working people have **less and less time** to spend with their families.*

We use *fewer* before a plural countable noun:
*Families are choosing to have **fewer children**.*

☆ In informal spoken English, many people also use *less* before a plural noun. This should not be used in written English, and will be marked as incorrect in formal written exams.

The opposite of both *less* and *fewer* is *more*: ***more** time / research / problems*

We also use *less / the least* before an adjective to form a negative comparative or superlative:
*Things are slightly **less expensive** here than in the capital.* (opposite *more expensive*)
*It's **the least common** of all the monkeys in the region.* (opposite *the most common*)

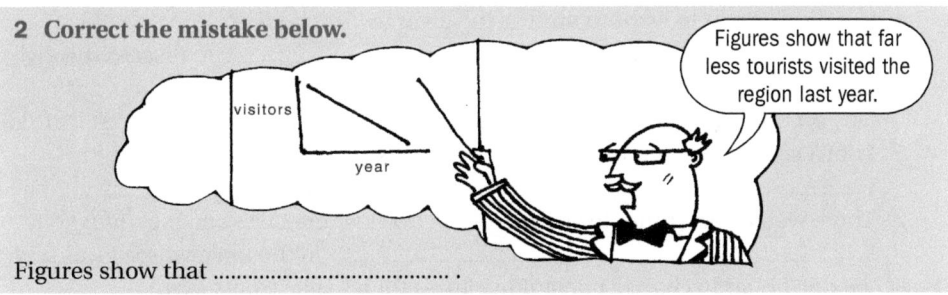

2 Correct the mistake below.

visitors

year

Figures show that far less tourists visited the region last year.

Figures show that ....

3 Complete the sentences below using *fewer, less* or *the least*.

1 There are .... jobs available for non-science graduates.
2 In urban areas there is .... affordable accommodation available.
3 The airline has cut costs and now has .... aircraft.
4 Our survey found that ironing was .... popular chore.
5 The resorts on the west coast are .... developed.
6 .... students are choosing to study History and Classics.
7 We encourage children to eat more fresh fruit and .... junk food.
8 Farmers are struggling because there's been .... rain this year than normal.

1 Complete the text using *a*, *the* or — .

Thirty years ago, this was quite (1) .... run-down neighbourhood and most of the families living here were (2) .... fairly poor. Over (3) .... last three decades, however, it has gradually become (4) .... more fashionable and (5) .... sort of place where (6) .... trendy young professionals now choose to live.

(7) .... main street has undergone (8) .... complete transformation, with greengrocers and butchers being replaced by fashion boutiques and hip cafés. It's also become one of (9) .... most popular nightspots in the city with (10) .... new bars and clubs opening on every street corner.

2 Complete the second sentence so that it has a similar meaning to the first sentence, using the word given.

1 Women can retire and receive a state pension when they are 60 years old. *(age)*
Women can retire and receive a state pension ....

2 There aren't as many independent record labels as there were 10 years ago. *(fewer)*
There .... there were 10 years ago.

3 They served beef in a fairly rich sauce. *(quite)*
They served beef ....

4 She didn't seem to want to discuss the divorce. *(impression)*
I .... to discuss the divorce.

5 Do you think it's true that the college is likely to close? *(really)*
Do you think .... to close?

6 I don't spend as much time with my family as I'd like. *(less)*
I .... I'd like.

7 There weren't any other foreigners in the town where I was staying. *(only)*
I .... in the town where I was staying.

8 We don't plan to change our staffing levels for a while. *(short term)*
We don't plan ....

9 She fell ill on Friday evening and was taken to hospital on Saturday. *(next)*
She fell ill ....

10 She chose the cheapest dish on the menu. *(expensive)*
She chose ....

3 Complete the conversation using one of the words from the box in each space. Each word is used only once.

> slightly   really   very   fewer   more   quite   less

Sam: What do you think of the new Chinese takeaway on the corner?

Clive: I think the food is (1) .... good. There are (2) .... dishes on the menu than you'd normally expect, but they seem (3) .... authentic than the other places I've tried.

Sam: Yes, I had some (4) .... good Sweet and Sour Chicken. I agree though that it is (5) .... a limited menu.

Clive: It's (6) .... more expensive than other takeaways, but you definitely pay (7) .... than you would in a restaurant.

4 Look at the charts and complete the sentences. Use one word in each space.

Bangkok Visitor Survey

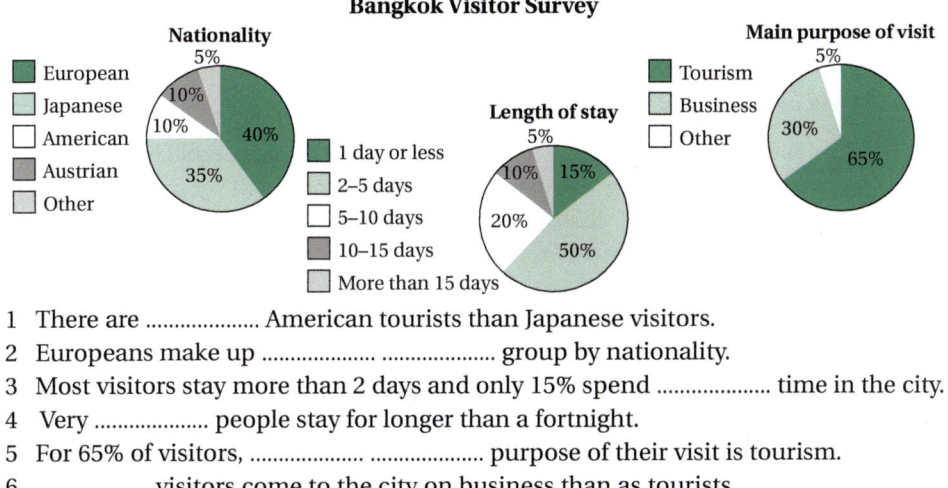

1 There are .... American tourists than Japanese visitors.
2 Europeans make up .... group by nationality.
3 Most visitors stay more than 2 days and only 15% spend .... time in the city.
4 Very .... people stay for longer than a fortnight.
5 For 65% of visitors, ... purpose of their visit is tourism.
6 .... visitors come to the city on business than as tourists.

5 Put the missing word in the correct place on the same line.

The World Health Organisation recommends that we eat five portions	
of fruit and vegetables a day as this amount contains minimum doses	*the*
of all the vitamins and minerals we need. It has been shown that people	
who eat the recommended intake suffer from minor illnesses. They are	*fewer*
also likely to be affected by some more serious conditions such as heart	*less*
disease and many types of cancer.	
Certain fruits and vegetables, such as avocados, blueberries and	
broccoli, contain high concentrations of certain nutrients, but the	*very*
important thing is to get plenty of variety. Fruit juice doesn't have all	*really*
the fibre of whole fruit, so only one portion a day should be in form of juice.	*the the*

Which preposition do I use after nouns?

1 Tick the correct sentence in each pair.

1 a We've seen a dramatic increase of air pollution in the city.
  b We've seen a dramatic increase in air pollution in the city.
2 a Only 36 students sat the exam, compared to 50 last year, a drop of 28%.
  b Only 36 students sat the exam, compared to 50 last year, a drop in 28%.

We use the preposition *in* after nouns to describe a measurable change:
- *a(n) increase / decrease*, etc. + *in* + noun (the thing which has changed):
  *There has been a sudden increase **in unemployment**.*

We use the preposition *of* to describe a general trend or the size of a change:
- *the rise / decline / increase*, etc. + *of* + noun:
  *His book investigates the **rise of trade unionism** in the region.* (general trend)
- *a(n) rise / increase / fall*, etc. + *of* + amount:
  *Only 56 turtles nested this year, **a fall of 20%** from last year.* (the size of the change)

Some uncountable nouns can only be followed by *of*:
*The **spread of** new technology has led to dramatic changes in the workplace.*

Growth is a difficult case. It usually follows the rules (*in* + measurable change, *of* + trend), but can be followed by either *of* or *in* in many contexts:
*the **growth in the number** of young people going to university*
*the **growth of interest** in renewable energies*

2 Correct the mistake below.

There has been a rapid increase of mobile phone ownership over the past 5 years.

phones

millions

time

There has been .... over the past 5 years.

3 Complete the following text using appropriate prepositions.

Not one area in England or Wales reported a fall (1) .... house prices last month, a survey has found. Cumbria saw the largest increase with an average rise (2) .... 1.5%. Prices show no sign of dropping despite recent rises (3) .... interest rates. Experts believe that the recent quarter point rise (4) .... 3.5% (5) .... 3.75% will do little to slow the market. Figures showed that there was also an increase last month (6) .... the number of sales (7) .... 3.3%. But at the start of this month, there was a fall (8) .... demand (9) .... 1.2% and a drop (10) .... 1.9% (11) .... the number of properties being put on the market.

Which preposition do I use after verbs?

1 Tick the correct sentence in each pair.

1. a An English breakfast consists bacon, eggs, sausage and tomato.
   b An English breakfast consists of bacon, eggs, sausage and tomato.
2. a Stop talking and concentrate on what you're doing.
   b Stop talking and concentrate in what you're doing.

Many verbs are usually followed by a particular preposition. You can check which preposition is used after a verb in a good learner's dictionary:

- *consist + of + (something)*:
  *The exam **consists of two parts**; a written test and an oral.* (not *consists in two parts*)
- *concentrate + on (doing) (something)*:
  *It's difficult to **concentrate on your work** with all this noise.*
  *I'd like to **concentrate** more **on improving** my writing skills.*
- *contribute + to + (something)*:
  *I'd like to thank everyone who **contributed to the success** of this project.*
- *depend + on + (someone / something)*:
  *The size of the grant you get **depends on your income**.* (not *depends of your income*)
- *insist + on + (doing) (something)*:
  *You should always **insist on a test drive** before buying a car.*
  *It was Joe who **insisted on bringing** a picnic.*

2 Correct the mistake below.

What are you going to wear for the wedding?

I'm not sure yet, it depends of the weather really.

I'm not sure yet, it ....

3 Complete the sentences with a verb + preposition from above.

1. You have to just ignore the crowd and .... the game.
2. If the goods are faulty you should.. a refund.
3. The visitor pack .... maps and guides to local attractions.
4. The cost of insurance will .... your age, driving record and type of car.
5. Scientists believe that carbon dioxide emissions .... global warming.
6. I think that the police should .... more .... preventing crime.
7. We all went out to dinner and Ben .... paying for the whole meal.
8. The President .... his advisers to keep him up-to-date with the facts.

By the time or at the time?

1 Tick the correct sentence in each pair.

1 a By the time we got there, the stadium was already full.
  b At the time we got there, the stadium was already full.
2 a At the time, I was a student, living in a tiny flat in London.
  b At the moment, I was a student, living in a tiny flat in London.

We use *by* when something has already happened before a particular time:
***By the time** the police arrived, the burglars had disappeared.* (the burglars left some time before the police arrived)
*I need to get this finished **by the end of the day**.* (before the end of the day)

At the time means 'then / when something was happening':
*Sarah was, in fact, already pregnant, but I didn't know that **at the time**.* (then)

We use *at that time* to emphasise that something was true then, but is different now:
***At that time**, he was just starting his acting career and was completely unknown.*
Also: *We had a test **at the end of** the course.* (e.g. in the last lesson)

At the moment means 'now or around now':
***At the moment**, I'm working on quite an interesting project.*

We use *at that moment* to refer to an exact time in the past, mostly in stories, when something happened suddenly:
*I wondered where Marie was and **at that moment**, the phone rang. It was her.*

2 Correct the mistake below.

Erm, I'm rather busy at the time. Can I call you back later?

I'm rather busy .... ?

3 Are these sentences right or wrong? Correct those which are wrong.

1 By the end of the show, everyone comes back on stage. ....
2 I have been to Paris before, but I was only ten at the moment. ....
3 By that time, my family were still living in Munich. ....
4 Don't worry – I'm sure they'll be back at the time it gets dark. ....
5 It was the only thing I could think of to say at the time. ....
6 It was in that moment that I realised the truth. ....
7 Where are you working at the moment? Still at the same place? ....
8 At midday his temperature had got worse, so I called the doctor. ....

22

1 Complete the newspaper cuttings with an appropriate preposition.

There has been a slump (1) .... almost 30% (2) .... package holiday sales for next summer. Bookings to Spain – the leading destination for inclusive holidays – have seen a drop (3) .... 35%.

The government is introducing a new system of fees for university students. Students will contribute (4) .... the cost of their education after they leave, with the size of the repayments depending (5) .... their level of income on graduation. The government say that the new charges are necessary because of the rapid growth (6) .... student numbers in recent years.

There has been a big leap (7) .... the number of women marrying younger men in the past 25 years, according to the Office for National Statistics. The proportion of brides marrying a younger man rose (8) .... 15% (9) .... 26% in the years from 1963 to 1998, it said. The report's authors said the findings were important because changing patterns (10) .... marital age gaps could have far-reaching implications for older couples. There could be fewer widows in future.

A new diet which promises weight loss (11) .... up to 5 kilos in just a couple of weeks has been criticised by health experts. According to the diet, each meal should consist (12) .... only one food type; vegetables, meat or fish.

2 Rewrite the sentences using the noun in brackets.

1 The company revealed that profits dropped by £1million last year. *(drop)*
   The company .... last year.

2 The campaign aims to stop AIDS spreading in the Developing World. *(spread)*
   The campaign .... in the Developing World.

3 Experts say that temperatures are rising by 1.5° per decade. *(rise)*
   Experts say .... per decade.

4 The number of people using mobile phones is growing rapidly. *(growth)*
   There is .... mobile phones.

5 Italians are unhappy that the standard of television has declined. *(decline)*
   Italians are .... television standards.

6 The treatment can lead to some patients gaining weight. *(gain)*
   The treatment .... some patients.

7 The agreement is aiming to reduce harmful emissions by 25%. *(reduction)*
   The agreement .... harmful emissions.

8 Over the past decade, we have seen sales decrease by 12%. *(decrease)*
   Over the past decade .... sales.

3 Complete the text using one preposition in each space.

Monday

(1) .... the end of last week, I came across a film crew filming a new movie with one of my favourite actors. I didn't have my camera with me (2) .... the time, so I rushed back to my car to get it. Unfortunately, (3) .... the time I got back, they'd finished the scene and the actor was nowhere to be seen. I was really disappointed and started walking back to my car when, just (4) .... that moment, he walked out of a building right there in front of me. I couldn't believe my luck – not only did I get to take his photo, but he gave me his autograph too!

4 Choose one word which can be used appropriately in both sentences.

1 She noticed she'd spilt a .... of red wine on her white shirt.
   We expect to see a .... in demand during the summer months.
2 Hang on, I'll be with you in just a ....
   I'm in a meeting at the .... Can I call you back in ten minutes?
3 My aunt had a nasty .... last week and broke her arm.
   There has been a slight .... in the cost of oil.
4 I was really tired and finding it difficult to ....
   Today, we're going to .... on improving your serve.
5 It was probably a mistake, but I was very young at the ....
   If you send it now, it should arrive in .... for his birthday.
6 What effect will the .... of MP3 have on the music industry?
   A child's diet should contain everything needed for healthy ....

5 Today is Monday. Look at the list of things to do and complete the text below using *by* or *at*.

'I'm really busy (1) .... the moment. Today, I need to have the final design for the new business cards ready (2) .... 11 o'clock, then I've got to go to pick up some dry cleaning (3) .... lunchtime. I've got a meeting first thing tomorrow, so I need to have everything prepared for that (4) .... the end of today. We need to discuss Phil's proposal and make a decision on it (5) .... tomorrow afternoon. Next year's brochures need to be ready (6) .... Thursday when Anna's coming in for them and I've got an important report to finish (7) .... the end of the week. Then we always have our regular team meeting (8) .... the end of the week – hopefully I'll have everything else finished (9) .... then. Oh yes, and I've got to remember to pick the car up from the garage (10) .... the weekend.'

Mon. 11 am – business cards to printers
Finish report before Fri.
Call Phil – Tues afternoon
Lunchtime – pick up dry cleaning
Meeting 9 am Tues.
Anna collecting brochures – Thurs.
Team meeting – Fri 3pm
Car ready – Saturday

Which nouns have irregular plural forms?

1 Tick the correct sentence in each pair.

1 a Why are we so interested in the lives of the rich and famous?
  b Why are we so interested in the lifes of the rich and famous?
2 a I met some really interesting persons on my travels.
  b I met some really interesting people on my travels.

Many common nouns have irregular or confusing plural forms:
- *life → lives* (also *wife → wives, knife → knives, roof → rooves*):
  *Do politicians really know anything about the **lives** of ordinary voters?*
- *belief → beliefs* (also *chief → chiefs*, but *thief → thieves*):
  *My parents both have very strong political **beliefs**.*
- *child → children*:
  *Many couples are choosing to have fewer **children**.*
- *aircraft → aircraft* (also *fish → fish, sheep → sheep*):
  *Local people complain about the noise of low-flying **aircraft**.*
- *person → people*:
  *We are campaigning for the rights of disabled **people**.*
  ☆ The plural form *persons* does exist, but is only used in legal or official contexts:
  *The law does not allow the sale of alcohol to **persons** under 18 years of age.*
- *baby → babies* (not ~~babys~~), *country → countries, family → families*, etc.
  ☆ Note: *story → stories* (a tale) but *storey → storeys* (a floor of a building):
  *He told me **stories** about his childhood.*   *a building with 5 **storeys***

2 Correct the mistake below.

Do you believe in life after death?

I'd rather not discuss my religious believes.

I'd rather ....

3 Complete the sentences using the singular or plural form of the nouns above.

1 Elderly .... complained that the new buses are difficult to get onto.
2 My grandfather spent his whole .... living in the same village.
3 The toy isn't suitable for .... under the age of five.
4 He suffered discrimination because of his political ....
5 No smoking is allowed on any of our ....
6 The vaccine could save the .... of thousands of ....
7 There is a widespread .... that diabetes is a genetic condition.
8 Both of my parents come from large .... , so I've got lots of aunts and uncles.

14 Everyday or every day?

1 Tick the correct sentence in each pair.

1 a Yoga can help you to cope with the stresses of every day life.
  b Yoga can help you to cope with the stresses of everyday life.
2 a I get nervous every time I get on a plane.
  b I get nervous everytime I get on a plane.

Every day, written as two separate words, means 'each day':
*I speak to my Mum on the phone almost **every day**.*

Everyday, written as one word, is an adjective meaning 'ordinary or normal'. It is always used before a noun:
*Schools should teach children skills they'll need in **everyday life**.*
*He painted pictures of **everyday objects**.*

Common compounds written as one word include:
everything, everywhere, everyone, everybody

But be careful:
***Everyone** agreed it was a good idea.* (all the people)
*The vases are handmade and **every one** is slightly different.* (each vase)
***Every time** we see him he seems to have a new problem.* (always two words)

2 Correct the mistake below.

Well, that's something you don't see everyday!

Well, that's .... !

3 Underline the correct word(s) in each sentence.

1 We receive hundreds of emails *everyday / every day*.
2 I get excited *everytime / every time* I see the team play.
3 I walk along this street *everyday / every day* and I'd never noticed that before.
4 I think *everybody / every body* enjoyed the party.
5 They rejected almost *everyone / every one* of his ideas.
6 The police asked *everyone / every one* to leave the building.
7 She's so good when it comes to practical, *everyday's / everyday* things.
8 I had a terrible day – *everything / every thing* seemed to go wrong.

15 How is British and American spelling different?

1 Tick the sentence in each pair which is correct in British English.

1 a The service is aimed mostly at business travelers.
  b The service is aimed mostly at business travellers.
2 a By the next day, the weather had gotten even worse.
  b By the next day, the weather had got even worse.

Many common words are spelt differently in British and American English. Although both forms are correct, you should not mix British and American spellings. In British examinations, American spellings will be marked as incorrect.

Some verbs ending in -*l* have a double -*l* before the ending in British English but a single -*l* in American English:
- *travelled → travelling* (also *traveller*) (UK); *traveled → traveling* (also *traveler*) (US)
- *cancelled → cancelling* (UK); *canceled → canceling* (US)

Also: *counsel, dial, equal, fuel, label, level, marvel, model, signal, total*
The past participle of *get* is different in British and American English:
- *get – got – got* (UK); *get – got – gotten* (US): *He's gotten used to living alone.* (US only)

Verbs which end -*ize* (UK & US), can also be spelt -*ise* in British English only:
- *organize → organise* (UK), *realize → realise* (UK), *analyze → analyse* (UK), etc.

Some past tense verbs which end -*ed* (UK & US) can also be spelt -*t* in British English:
- *learned → learnt* (UK), *spelled → spelt* (UK), *spoiled → spoilt* (UK), etc.

2 Make the sentence below correct in British English.

LONDON ✈ HEATHROW
UK PASSPORT CONTROL
**PASSENGERS TRAVELING FROM OUTSIDE THE EUROPEAN UNION
MUST COMPLETE A LANDING CARD**

.... outside the European Union must complete a landing card.

3 Make sentences 1–4 correct in British English and 5–8 in American English.

1 Only products from certain farms can be labeled organic. ....
2 Johnson equaled the fastest time ever for the event. ....
3 Planes have gotten bigger as air travel has increased. ....
4 The hotel is just a few hundred meters from the beach. ....
5 There has been a quick reaction from international aid organisations. ....
6 He learnt Spanish while he was travelling in Latin America. ....
7 She'd had her hair cut short and I didn't recognise her at first. ....
8 It's difficult to remember how some words are spelt. ....

TEST 5

1 Complete the following spelling rules.

1 .... is an adjective meaning 'ordinary or normal' which is always used .... a noun.

2 The normal plural form of *person* is .... The more formal plural form, ... , is only used in legal and .... contexts.

3 Nouns which end in the letter -*y* usually take the plural ending .... ; the word .... is an exception.

4 In British English, the past participle of the verb *to get* is .... but in American English, the past participle .... is also used.

5 Some verbs ending in .... in British English have a double consonant in the past tense. In American English, there is only ....

2 Complete the pairs of sentences in British or American English.

'Our flight was cancelled because the (1) .... developed a fault.'

'Our flight was (2) .... because the airplane developed a fault.'

'We were travelling along the motorway when a bird hit the windscreen.'

'We were (3) .... along the freeway when a bird hit the windshield.'

'I didn't realise so many words could be (4) .... differently in the US.'

'I didn't (5) .... so many words could be spelled differently in the UK.'

'Steve really has got fatter since he started work at the sweet shop.'

'Steve sure has (6) .... fatter since he started work at the candy store.'

In most cultures, danger is signalled by the (7) .... red.

In most cultures, danger is (8) .... by the color red.

3 There are eight spelling mistakes and four American spellings in this British English text. Correct the mistakes and change the spellings to British English.

> Last year, I visited Latin America for the first time. I started off in Lima, the capital of Peru. It was fascinating to explore the city and get a glimpse into the every day lifes of the persons living there. I visited some of the poorer suburbs where many familys live in small one- or two-room houses with tin roofs. Every one was really friendly though, especially the childs. Then I traveled on to Cusco, one of the highest cities in the world at 3,350 meters, to get ready for the highlight of my trip – a 5-day hike along the Inca Trail to Machu Picchu. Lots of travelers spend a few days there until they've gotten used to the altitude before starting the hike. I met some really interesting people and heard lots of amazing storys about their adventures.

4 Complete the following dictionary definitions from the *Cambridge Advanced Learner's Dictionary* with words from units 14 and 15.

(1) .... *noun* [C] *plural* (2) ....
the woman to whom a man is married
(3) .... *noun* [C] *plural* (4) ....
any vehicle, with or without an engine, which can fly, such as a plane or helicopter
(5) .... *verb* [I or T] *past tense* (6) .... or US
USUALLY (7) ....
to make a movement, sound, flash, etc. which gives information or tells people what to do
(8) ...., US USUALLY (9) .... *noun* [C]
someone who is trained to listen to people and give them advice about their problems

5 Use the word at the start of the line to form a word that fits in the space on the same line.

life	Recent heavy rains across the south of France have brought widespread flooding, disrupting the (1) .... of thousands of
person	(2) .... For many, losing their homes and possessions has been a traumatic experience and the authorities have
counsel	(3) .... working in the temporary shelters to cope with the psychological as well as the practical effects of this disaster. Transport
cancel	has been severely disrupted with many trains (4) .... and
aircraft	a number of (5) .... stranded at Nice airport which has
travel	been totally cut off by the floods. (6) .... are advised to contact train operators or airlines for more information.

16 Which phrasal verbs are formed with *stand*?

1 Tick the correct sentence in each pair.

1 a We had to stand up at 6 am to start the trek.
   b We had to get up at 6 am to start the trek.
2 a He should stand up to what he believes in.
   b He should stand up for what he believes in.

Many phrasal verbs are very similar in form, but have different meanings.

- *stand up* means 'move from a sitting position to a standing position':
  *The children all **stand up** when the teacher comes in the classroom.*
- *get up* means 'get out of bed':
  *I usually **get up** at about eight o'clock.*
- *stand up for your beliefs, rights* etc. means 'defend something you believe in':
  *Union leaders encouraged the workers to **stand up for their rights**.*
- *stand up for (someone)* means 'defend someone who is being criticised':
  *Lucy was the only one who **stood up for me**.*
- *stand by your beliefs / your principles / your decision* means 'not change your mind':
  *His family are **standing by their decision** to go ahead with the operation.*
- *stand in for (someone)* means 'do someone's job for them when they are not there':
  *Your normal teacher is sick today, so I'm **standing in for her**.*

2 Correct the mistake below.

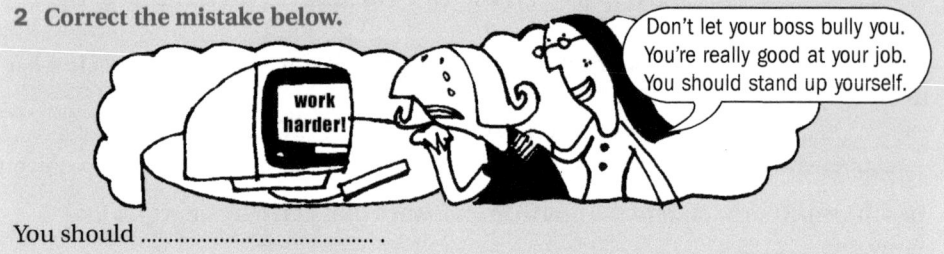

work harder!

Don't let your boss bully you. You're really good at your job. You should stand up yourself.

You should ....

3 Complete the sentences using one or more preposition.

1 I'm really busy today; could you stand .... me at the meeting?
2 She stood .... her husband throughout the trial, claiming he was completely innocent.
3 Women are becoming more politically aware and standing .... their rights.
4 She stood .... to offer her seat to an old lady.
5 He was jailed just because he stood .... his beliefs.
6 I stand .... what I said before. I still believe it's the right thing to do.
7 Johnson is injured, so Wilkinson is standing .... him as captain.
8 Despite pressure from the media, the sport's governing body is standing .... its decision to suspend him.

Which phrases are formed with *take*?

1 Tick the correct sentence in each pair.

1 a The wedding took place in a small village church.
  b The wedding took part in a small village church.

2 a You have to take in account how much you can afford.
  b You have to take into account how much you can afford.

Take is used in many common phrases which are often confused:
- *take part in (something)* means 'participate in an event':
  *Teams from all over the world will **take part in the championships**.*
- *take place* means 'happen':
  *The next World Championships will **take place in South Africa**.*

Be careful to choose the correct preposition in these phrases:
- *take care of (something)* means 'deal with something':
  *I'll meet you later, I've got **a few things** to **take care of** in the office first.*
- *take care of (someone)* means 'look after someone (e.g. a baby, child or sick person)':
  *Maria has to **take care of her younger brothers and sisters**.* (not ~~take care about~~)
- *take (something) into account / consideration* means 'consider something (when making a decision)':
  ***The concerns** of local residents should be **taken into account**.* (not ~~taken in account~~)
  Also: *take a step / a chance / a risk*:
  *We should **take steps** to cut pollution.*
  *Anelka isn't playing. He can't afford to **take the risk** of getting injured again.*

2 Correct the mistake below.

I'm quite ....

3 Are the sentences right or wrong? Correct any mistakes.

1 Lots of celebrities took place in the charity race. ....
2 Don't worry, I'll take care of all the travel arrangements. ....
3 Angela screamed and made a step back. ....
4 Children should be encouraged to take participation in sporting activities.
  ....
5 The meeting will take part in the town hall next week. ....
6 I'm sure Greg's old enough to take care about himself now. ....
7 You're taking a risk investing all your money in this project. ....
8 You can borrow my bike, but please take a good care of it. ....

31

18 Commonly confused word forms

1 Tick the correct sentence in each pair.

1 a The kids were tired and beginning to lose interest.

   b The kids were tired and beginning to loose interest.

2 a The sun always raises in the East.

   b The sun always rises in the East.

Be careful not to confuse the noun *loss*, the verb form *lose* and the adjective *loose*.

- *loss* /lɒs/ (plural *losses*):
  *These factory closures will result **in the loss** of thousands of jobs.*
- *lose* /luːz/ – *lost* – *lost*:
  *Thousands of jobs will be **lost** as a result of these factory closures.*
  Also: *lose interest / patience* (become bored / impatient), *lose confidence / faith*
- *loose* /luːs/ (adjective meaning 'not tight'):
  *You should wear **loose**, comfortable clothing.*

Be careful not to confuse the intransitive verb *rise* and the transitive verb *raise*:

- *rise* – *rose* – *risen* (verb) means 'to go up or increase':
  *Experts are predicting that fuel costs will **rise**.*
- We also use the verb *raise* (– *raised* – *raised*) when someone increases something:
  *The new government is planning to **raise** taxes.*
  Also: *raise children* (bring them up), *raise doubts / fears, raise a question / problem*
- *rise* (noun): *Experts are predicting **a rise** in the cost of fuel.*

☆ The noun *raise* is mostly American English and means 'an increase in wages':
*I asked my boss for **a raise**. (UK: I asked my boss for **a pay rise**.)*

2 Correct the mistake below.

You look loss. Can I help?

.... Can I help?

3 Complete the sentences using the correct form of one of the words above.

1 The number of accidents caused by drunk drivers has .... dramatically.

2 My neighbour has a key to my flat just in case I .... mine.

3 We'd already been waiting 2 hours and were .... patience.

4 Unemployment .... to 9.4% last month.

5 After several bad results, he .... confidence in his ability.

6 After a bad year the company announced .... this year.

7 The disease can cause confusion and .... of memory.

8 Some people have .... doubts about the safety of the factory.

TEST 6

1 Complete the second sentence so that it has the same meaning as the first, using the word in brackets.

1 There has been a 5% rise in accommodation costs in the past 3 years. *(risen)*
Accommodation costs .... in the past 3 years.

2 Many factors need to be considered when choosing a site for a new school. *(account)*
Many factors .... when choosing a site for a new school.

3 Don't worry, the nurses will look after you while you're in hospital. *(care)*
Don't worry, the nurses .... while you're in hospital.

4 These people do not want to bring their children up in a refugee camp. *(raise)*
These people .... in a refugee camp.

5 Many illnesses can cause you to lose your appetite. *(loss)*
Many illnesses can ....

6 I always have trouble getting up on a Monday morning. *(bed)*
I always have trouble .... on a Monday morning.

7 We will hold the next conference in Brighton next April. *(place)*
The next conference .... next April.

8 An understudy is someone who replaces a stage actor if they are ill. *(stand)*
An understudy .... if they are ill.

2 Complete the texts below using one word in each space.

Tennis player Martina Williams has announced that she will not take (1) .... in the Australian Open which takes (2) .... in Sydney next month. She hasn't played since she (3) .... in the semi-finals of the French Open last year. Her withdrawal has (4) .... new doubts about her fitness, but her coach told reporters yesterday that her recovery from knee surgery is going well. 'She's doing well, but she doesn't want to (5) .... the risk of coming back too quickly and getting injured.'

The English cricket manager has come in for criticism over his team selection after the team (6) .... their recent Test Match against India. Some commentators have (7) .... questions about whether Wilson should have been selected as captain, but the manager is (8) .... by his decision and will not change the line-up for the next game in Pakistan.

3 Read the notices and complete the sentences using the correct form of the word or phrase in brackets.

CHARITY FUN RUN
Bristol ~ 9 April
Application forms available
from Sports Centre

PUBLIC MEETING
Your chance to ask
questions about the
proposed road and put
forward your opinion.

Protest March – May 1
No to job cuts!
Yes to workers' rights!

1 The fun run .... on 9 April. *(take place)*
2 The run is to .... for charity. *(raise)*
3 Anyone who .... from the sports centre. *(take part)*
4 At the public meeting, people .... questions about the new road. *(raise)*
5 The opinions of local people .... *(consideration)*
6 A protest march .... on 1 May. *(take place)*
7 People are protesting .... *(loss)*
8 The protesters are .... workers' rights. *(stand up for)*

4 Complete the texts below using one preposition in each space.

Rosa gets (1) .... at six o'clock every morning to take her children to their grandparents, who take care (2) .... them while she's at work. She would like to stay at home and look (3) .... the children herself but she can't afford to. The huge rise (4) .... the cost of living in the past few years has forced her to go back to work.

Olivier has been in a wheelchair since the loss (5) .... his right leg in an accident two years ago. He now spends much of his time standing up (6) .... the rights of disabled people. He says that many organisations don't take the needs of disabled people (7) .... account when designing public buildings. He says that lack of access prevents disabled people from taking part (8) .... many everyday activities that able-bodied people take for granted.

5 Match 1–5 and a–e to make sentences.

1 I'll book the flights if you take ....   a   steps to ban drugs.
2 When Helen's not here, I stand ....   b   up all day.
3 Alison raised   c   any risks.
4 I'm really tired from standing ....   d   care of the hotel.
5 It's probably a false alarm, but we can't take ....   e   in for her.
6 The attack raised ....   f   the question of compensation.
7 The sport is taking ....   g   up for me.
8 The teacher didn't believe me, but Jo stood ....   h   fears of renewed violence.

Way, route, means or method?

1 Tick the correct sentence in each pair.

1. a Do you know the planned way of the new rail line?
   b Do you know the planned route of the new rail line?
2. a Travel is a great way to broaden the mind.
   b Travel is a great method to broaden the mind.

We use *way* to refer generally to directions from one place to another:
*Can you tell me **the way to the station**?*

We use *route* to refer to a journey from one place to another, the roads you use, etc.:
*She always **takes the same route** to work.*

We use *path* to describe how you get from one situation to another:
*After leaving school, the two brothers' careers followed quite different **paths**.*

We use *way*, *means* and *method* to say how you do something. *Means* and *method* are used mainly in written language. *Method* is mostly used to describe technical procedures, such as in science, finance, etc.:

* *way + to do (something): He showed me the best **way to clean** the windows.*
* *way + of doing (something): What's the quickest **way of getting** to the airport?*
* *method + of + noun / doing (something): a leaflet about **methods of birth control***
* *means + of + noun / doing (something): Email is our main **means of contact**.*
  ☆ *Means* is both the singular and plural form:
  *The congestion charge is **a means of cutting** traffic. (not ~~a mean of cutting traffic~~)*
  *There are **several different means of calculating** the distance.*

2 Correct the mistake below.

> What do you think is the best means to study for the exam?

What do you think is the best .... for the exam?

3 Underline the correct noun in each sentence.

1. Police and organisers disagreed about the *way / route* of the parade.
2. We need to look into alternative *ways / methods* of waste disposal.
3. I had an accident on my *way / path* to work.
4. People in rural areas drive because there isn't any other *way / means* of transport.
5. Are written exams the best *way / method* of assessment for language students?
6. It's a good *way / means* to get started in the sport.
7. On a Friday evening, there's always heavy traffic on all *ways / routes* out of the city.
8. Music can be an important *way / means* of expression for children.

20 Work or job?

1 Tick the correct sentence in each pair.

1 a I'm lucky to have a job which I enjoy.
  b I'm lucky to have a work which I enjoy.
2 a How long is your journey to work?
  b How long is your journey to your job?

Work is an uncountable noun which we use to describe the things you do to earn money or to achieve something, or the place where you work:
*I'll be home late tonight, I've got **a lot of work** to finish.*
*What time do you **start / finish work**?*
*I take the kids to school in the morning before I **go to work**.* (go to my office, etc.)
*Is there a number I can call you on **at work**?* (at your office etc.)
*Many of the young men in the village are **out of work**.* (unemployed)

Job is a countable noun which we use to describe a particular position you have working for a company:
*When he left college, he **got a job** in a bank.*
*Her father **lost his job**.* (became unemployed)

We use *career* to describe all the jobs you have in your life, often in one area of work:
*My parents tried to discourage me from **a career in journalism**.*

2 Correct the mistake below.

I wish I had a more interesting work.

I wish I had ....

3 Complete the text using one word from above in each space.

Whilst more young women than ever before are now pursuing (1) ....
in law, business and other professions, they are struggling to find the right balance
between (2) .... and family life. If they don't want to give up a
good (3) .... when they have a baby, many women find themselves
pressured to return to (4) .... as soon as possible after maternity
leave. Women with school-age children also face problems juggling a busy
(5) .... and domestic commitments. The long hours demanded
in many top (6) .... mean starting (7) .... early
and finishing late, missing out on valuable time with children. Taking too much time
off (8) .... to look after sick children can also damage women's
chances of promotion compared to their male colleagues.

21 Commonly confused nouns: *relation* / *relationship*, *education* / *upbringing*

1 Tick the correct sentence in each pair.

1 a I've always had a close relation with my grandparents.
    b I've always had a close relationship with my grandparents.
2 a My father was often away and didn't really play a part in my upbringing.
    b My father was often away and didn't really play a part in my education.

We use *relationship* to describe:
* the way people feel and behave towards each other – friends, colleagues, family:
  *He has / doesn't have **a** very good **relationship with his boss**.* (not ~~relationship to~~)
* the family connection between two people:
  *What's her **relationship to you**? She's my aunt.*

A *relation* or a *relative* is a member of your family:
*He's **a distant relation**.*   *a party for friends and **relatives***

We use *relations* (always plural) to describe the way two groups of people, countries etc., behave towards each other and communicate:
*public / industrial / international / diplomatic **relations***
***Relations between the two countries** have improved.*

We use *education* to describe what someone learns in school, college, etc., and *upbringing* for what we learn from parents and family about how to behave:
*Many of the children in this remote village receive no formal **education**.*
*I came from a Catholic family and had a strict, religious **upbringing**.*

2 Correct the mistake below.

This agreement can only improve the trade relationship between our two nations.

This agreement can only improve ....

3 Complete the sentences with one word from above.

1 She seemed to have a good .... with her parents.
2 I've got some .... who live in Australia who I've never met.
3 The two governments have broken off diplomatic ....
4 It was her first serious .... and she was upset when they split up.
5 There's always a special .... between a mother and baby.
6 In many cultures, women are responsible for children's ....
7 .... between workers and management had reached a low point.
8 The government has promised to spend more on health and ....

1 Complete the sentences using a word from the box. Each word is used once.

job	work	means	journey	method	way	ways	route

Transport survey

Commuters:

How far do you travel to (1) .... ?

Which (2) .... of transport do you use?

Do you always take the same (3) .... ?

How long does your (4) .... take?

Do you ever read / use a laptop / make phone calls on your
(5) .... to work?

Business travellers:

Do you have to travel abroad as part of your (6) .... ?

What do you find are the best (7) .... of combating jetlag?

When travelling abroad what (8) .... of payment do you use?
(credit card / cash, etc.)

2 Choose one word which can be used appropriately in both sentences.

1 Some people said the minister's visit was just a public ....
exercise.

The trade dispute has soured .... between America and the EU.

2 She was injured in an accident at ....

Many people move to the capital city to look for ....

3 Which .... do we go now – right or left?

Joining a sports club is a great .... to meet new people.

4 Mum gave me the .... of chopping up all the vegetables.

I think Helena starts her new .... on Monday.

5 What's the best .... of treatment for the disease?

The main teaching .... used at the university is the traditional
lecture.

6 We're not friends outside the office, but we have a good working
....

She's not married, but is in a long-term ....

7 The fire burnt out of control, destroying everything in its ....

It was a long, hard .... towards independence for the tiny state.

8 I have .... all over the world.

She took on the responsibility of caring for an elderly ....

3 Are these sentences right or wrong? Correct any that are wrong.

1 Being the youngest of seven brothers and sisters was a major factor in my bringing up.

....

2 Both brothers have a very close relationship to their father. ....

3 I first met my husband in work. ....

4 The airlines compete for the most lucrative transatlantic routes. ....

5 Many people find debit cards the most convenient method to pay. ....

6 There has been an improvement in relations of the government and unions.

....

7 The scheme is to help people who've been out of job for more than 6 months.

....

8 I'd like to pursue a career in marine biology. ....

4 Complete the following newspaper cuttings, using one word from units 19–21 in each space.

When Tamara Stein met Louisa Scott in the parking lot of a local McDonald's, their lives changed forever. The two New York students share a birthday, are exactly the same height and they both love hip-hop. More importantly they share a (1) .... – a Mexican mother who gave them up for adoption in the US at birth. Although they grew up just 20 miles apart, they had quite different (2) .... ; Tamara was raised in a Jewish Manhattan family, while Louisa grew up Catholic in suburban Long Island. The twins are now finishing their studies; getting a good (3) .... is important to both of them, and they're both contemplating a (4) .... in the music business. 'I can't believe our (5) .... have never crossed before,' says Tamara. 'I feel she's my sister, but our (6) .... right now is more as friends.'

Have you ever thought of a (7) .... in civil engineering? Look around your own area at the bridges, shopping centres, leisure facilities and transport provision to appreciate how the (8) .... of civil engineers contributes to your daily life. When you start (9) .... as a civil engineer, you can expect to be paid around £18,000. What you earn as you work your way up the (10) .... ladder depends on the (11) .... you take and how committed you are to the (12) ....

Three buses powered by hydrogen are to be introduced on (13) .... in central London. London is one of nine European cities participating in a two-year trial of this new cleaner (14) .... of transport as part of a European scheme to reduce pollution. London Transport have chosen to trial the new buses on several busy (15) .... used by commuters travelling to and from (16) .... in Central London.

Commonly confused adjectives: *tourist* / *touristic*, *economic* / *economical*

1 Tick the correct sentence in each pair.

1 a Money should be spent on restoring these important touristic places.
  b Money should be spent on restoring these important tourist attractions.
2 a The country faces various economical and social problems.
  b The country faces various economic and social problems.

Tourist is a noun which refers to people who visit a place on holiday:
*There are many **tourists** in Cambridge at this time of year.*

We use *tourist* as an adjective, particularly in a number of common phrases:
- the **tourist** industry / trade, **tourist** information / office / board
- a **tourist** attraction (a place which tourists like to visit, e.g. a church, castle, etc.)
- **tourist** / **holiday** destination (an area, town, etc. popular with tourists)
- **tourist** / **holiday** resort (a town where the main business is *tourism*, often by the sea)

We can use the adjective *touristy* to describe a place which we feel has too many tourists and is too commercialised. It is negative, informal and usually spoken:
*I don't want to go somewhere too **touristy**.*   *stalls selling **touristy** souvenirs*

Economic is an adjective, usually used before a noun, to describe something related to the economy of a country or organisation: *economic growth / policy / problem*

Economical describes something that saves you money, especially by using less fuel etc. than normal: *More people are now opting for smaller, more **economical** cars.*

2 Correct the mistake below.

> This year's bad weather has really affected touristic businesses.

This year's bad weather has ....

3 Underline the most appropriate phrase to complete each sentence.

1 Paris is one of the most popular tourist *destinations* / *resorts* in the world.
2 There has been an increase in the popularity of environmental *tourist* / *tourism*.
3 This tiny island relies on tourism for its *economical* / *economic* survival.
4 We did a tour of the main *sightseeing places* / *tourist attractions* around the city.
5 The local bars and restaurants are full during the *touristic* / *holiday* season.
6 Unemployment is caused by an unstable *economic* / *economy*.
7 This printer's unique ink refill system makes it very *economic* / *economical* to run.
8 *Touristical growth* / *The growth of tourism* has brought new jobs to the area.

Common, ordinary or usual?

1 **Tick the correct sentence in each pair.**

1 a His books make science interesting to ordinary people.
  b His books make science interesting to common people.
2 a He points out some of the most common errors made by new skiers.
  b He points out some of the most usual errors made by new skiers.

We use *common* to describe something which happens or exists very often or in many places, situations, etc.:
*Homelessness is **a common problem** in big cities.*
*It's very **common** now for children to have TVs in their bedroom.*

To describe a person as *common* can have negative connotations about being poor, unimportant or uneducated. We use *ordinary* or *average* to describe a person:
*His neighbours said that he seemed like a very **ordinary person**.*
*This type of luxury resort is out of the price range of **the average person**.*

We use *usual* to describe something you normally do or expect to happen:
*I'll meet you at the park at **the usual time**.* (the time you meet every day / week)

We also use several other words in certain fixed collocations:
*I first met my boyfriend via **a mutual friend**.* (a friend of both people)
*We became friends through our **shared interest** in hiking.* (we both enjoy it)
*The team line-up is **a joint decision** between the coach and the captain.*

2 Correct the mistake below.

> We met last year in Hong Kong when we were introduced by a common friend.

We were introduced ....

3 **Complete the sentences with one of the adjectives above.**

1 The film is about three girls with a .... passion for music.
2 These little lizards are very .... in Southern Europe.
3 I parked my car in the .... place, just round the corner from my office.
4 She's just a(n) .... teenager, studying at her local college.
5 It's quite .... for students to have a part-time job.
6 She was given Alex's address by a .... friend.
7 Politicians are often thought to be out of touch with .... people.
8 Neck and back injuries are very .... among rugby players.

24 *Important, relevant* or *essential*?

1 Tick the correct sentence in each pair.

1 a Food is a very important part of the culture of a country.
  b Food is a very vital part of the culture of a country.
2 a Light and water are essential for all plants to grow.
  b Light and water are relevant for all plants to grow.

Important is a common adjective: *I have some **very important** questions to ask him.*
It is often confused with other similar adjectives, which have slightly different
meanings and may occur in strong collocations:

- *significant* means 'noticeable, worth thinking about or having an effect on something':
  *There's been **a significant increase** in the number of foreign students.*
- *relevant* means 'connected with or appropriate for what is being discussed':
  *When you come to the embassy, make sure you bring all the **relevant documents**.*
  *I don't see how that's **relevant to** my application.*
- *crucial / vital / essential* means 'necessary and more important than anything else':
  *It's **essential to** book in advance if you want a good seat.*
- *fundamental* means 'forming the basis of something (and so extremely important)':
  *There have been **fundamental changes** to the way we work.*

☆ These are 'limit' adjectives and are not normally used with *very / quite / more*, etc.
To emphasise the adjective, you can use *absolutely vital / essential*, etc.:
It's absolutely essential to start off with a good business plan. (not *it's very essential*)

2 Correct the mistake below.

The right equipment is very essential as the weather can change very quickly up here.

The right equipment .... as the weather can change very quickly.

3 Underline the most appropriate adjective to complete each of the sentences.

1 It is *vital / fundamental* that we get him to hospital right away.
2 Good communication is the most *important / necessary* thing in a relationship.
3 There has been no *important / significant* change in the patient's condition.
4 For more information, see the *relevant / essential* pages of the manual.
5 I've got a(n) *vital / important* meeting with my assistant this afternoon.
6 It's very *essential / important* to make sure the power is switched off first.
7 'Innocent until proved guilty' is a *fundamental / crucial* principle of British law.
8 Some pupils feel that subjects like history aren't *significant / relevant* to their lives.

TEST 8

1 Match the adjectives (1–5) and nouns (a–h) which fit best together to make phrases.

1	a joint	a	part of our culture
2	a popular holiday	b	person
3	quite a common	c	destination
4	a shared	d	industry
5	a vital	e	friend
6	the tourist	f	decision
7	an ordinary	g	interest in green issues
8	a mutual	h	problem for language learners

2 The following text contains 10 errors. Find the errors and correct them.

Boredom is the most usual cause of pupils losing interest in school, says the Education Minister.

'A big minority of young people, especially boys, get turned off in secondary school soon after they arrive. If I had to pick out a fundamentally reason why this minority get turned off, I would have no hesitation: boredom.'

Speaking at a conference, the minister said that boredom was at the root of many discipline problems. He said that it was essential for schools alter their approach to teaching and to make the curriculum more relevant for the everyday lives of common young people.

'It is very vital that we connect with young people and teach them the skills that they believe will be the important to them in their adult lives. We need to hook into what motivates the normal teenager and build on that.'

The government's proposals to help tackle this problem include an increased role for vocational training and a significantly increase in the use of information technology.

3 Replace the word or phrase in italics in each sentence with a synonym from the box. Make any other small changes that are necessary.

> joint   significant   relevant   usual
> essential average   common   fundamental

1 It's becoming almost impossible for an *ordinary* young couple to get a foot on the property ladder now. ....

2 There hasn't been any *noticeable* change in his condition since last night. ....

3 The right to food and water is a *basic* human right. ....

4 The procedure *we normally use* is to ask for two items of identification. ....

5 It isn't *absolutely necessary* to describe every little detail, just the main points. ....

6 It's still *not unusual* for widows in Greece to dress all in black. ....

7 Where we go on holiday is usually a decision *made by both of us*. ....

8 And how is that *connected with* the murder investigation? ....

4 Use the 'across' and 'down' clues to complete this crossword.

Across →
1 a town by the sea for tourists
4 not as tight
6 what you hope to have on holiday!
7 very important
11 another time
12 type of industry or business
13 very important

Down ↓
2 the place you are going to
3 over-commercialised for tourists
5 connected to something
6 basic and very important
8 happening most of the time
9 not unusual, special or different to others
10 like most people or things

When do I use an adverb or an adjective?

1 Tick the correct sentence in each pair.

1 a We had to get used to a new home and a complete different culture.
   b We had to get used to a new home and a completely different culture.
2 a There aren't any easy solutions to this problem.
   b There aren't any easily solutions to this problem.

Complete, absolute, relative, etc. are adjectives and are usually used before a noun:
The whole evening was a(n) complete / absolute disaster!
I didn't know anyone – they were all total strangers. (not ~~totally strangers~~)

Clear, different, easy, simple, etc. are also adjectives and can be used before a noun or
after the verbs *be / look / sound / taste / smell / feel / seem* to describe a noun:
It was a simple / easy mistake to make.
John is very different from his brother. (*different* describes John)

Completely, absolutely, relatively, etc. are adverbs and are usually used before an
adjective or past participle (*ruined, covered, confused* etc.):
It's a relatively quiet area.   The carpet was absolutely / completely ruined.
They're from completely different generations. (not ~~complete different generations~~)

Clearly, differently, easily, simply, etc. are adverbs and are usually used with a verb to
describe the way someone does something:
You shouldn't give up so easily.   People from different cultures think differently.

2 Correct the mistake below.

Sorry, can you explain that again more simple?

Sorry, can you .... ?

3 Complete the text using the correct form of the words in italics.

Last February, I visited a friend in New York. One evening, it started
snowing, (1) .... at first and then more   *gentle*
(2) .... Next morning, everywhere was   *heavy*
(3) .... covered in a (4) ....   *complete   thick*
blanket of snow. We put on plenty of (5) ....   *warm*
clothes and went out to explore. The streets seemed very
(6) .... as there was no traffic. The snowstorm had   *quiet*
brought one of the (7).. cities in the world to a   *busy*
(8) .... standstill!   *complete*

1 Tick the correct sentence in each pair.

1 a Traffic congestion is a serious problem, specially in big cities.
  b Traffic congestion is a serious problem, especially in big cities.
2 a The police especially want to speak to anyone who witnessed the attack.
  b Especially, the police want to speak to anyone who witnessed the attack.

Usually, *especially* means 'particularly' and *specially* means 'for a particular purpose':
*I love Italian food, **especially** pasta.* (not *specially pasta*)
*a car **specially** designed for cities*

In many situations, the two words are used with the same meaning:
*I've made chocolate cake **specially / especially** for you.*

Specially is mostly used with an adjective made from a past participle: *specially designed / trained / prepared* etc. It is not used at the beginning of a sentence or phrase: *a **specially-built** stadium*
*The stadium was **built specially** for the Olympic Games.* (built for that purpose)

Especially is often used at the beginning of a phrase (often after a comma) or before a verb, but not at the beginning of a sentence:
*There's been a lot of flooding, **especially** in the south.*
*I **especially** liked the big balcony.* (not *Especially I liked ...*)

It's also used before an adjective for emphasis: *especially difficult / important*, etc.:
*The chocolate cake was **especially good**.* (very good, better than the other cakes)

2 Correct the mistake below.

I enjoy especially baking cakes and biscuits.

.... cakes and biscuits.

3 Are these sentences right or wrong? Correct any that are wrong.

1 I don't like driving at night, specially if it's raining. ....
2 The police use specially-trained dogs to search for drugs. ....
3 Especially women should be careful when travelling alone. ....
4 Malaria is still a big problem, specially in parts of Africa. ....
5 I drive a car which especially is designed for disabled drivers. ....
6 These exhibits were especially popular among children. ....
7 Especially the museum is renowned for its collection of modern art. ....
8 Is it just me or is it specially cold today? ....

Eventually or finally?

1 Tick the correct sentence in each pair.

1 a If we don't act now, the rainforests will eventually be destroyed.
   b If we don't act now, the rainforests will finally be destroyed.
2 a Eventually, I would like to thank all the staff for their hard work.
   b Finally, I would like to thank all the staff for their hard work.

We use *finally* to introduce the last thing in a series of actions, points or arguments. When used like this, it always comes at the beginning of the phrase or sentence:
*Mix together the oil and vinegar, add some herbs and **finally**, season with salt.*
*Firstly … Secondly … **Finally**, we must recognise that …*

We use both *finally* and *eventually* to describe something that happened only after a long time or after a lot of effort, work, etc.:
*After months of looking, he **finally** / **eventually** found a job.*

Both are used at the beginning of a phrase, or before the verb (but after an auxiliary):
***Finally**, the building work was finished. The building work was **finally** finished.*
***Eventually**, we reached the border. We **eventually** reached the border.*

Eventually can also be used at the end of sentence:
*We reached the border **eventually**.*

2 Correct the mistake below.

He took ages filling in the form. Then he told me that I'd passed finally!

Then ....

3 Complete the sentences using *finally*, *eventually*, *actually*, *eventual* or *possible*.

1 With more research, I'm sure we will find a cure ....
2 We should consider how we will deal with any .... problems.
3 I've spoken to him on the phone, but we've never .... met.
4 .... , I will discuss the practical applications of this research.
5 The bolts were very tight, but we got them undone ....
6 No one yet knows what the .... outcome will be.
7 She kept searching and .... found the key under a pile of books.
8 He had a succession of injuries. First, it was his knee, then his shoulder and
   .... he suffered a broken ankle which ended his career.

1 Complete the second sentence so that it has a similar meaning to the first sentence, using the given word.

1 I don't think that his story was the complete truth. *(completely)*
I don't think that ....

2 In the end, we got to the hotel around midnight. *(finally)*
We .... around midnight.

3 Disabled people take part in the race in wheelchairs made for the purpose. *(specially)*
Disabled people .... wheelchairs.

4 Everyone stood there without saying a single word. *(absolute)*
Everyone ....

5 He gave us instructions which were unambiguous. *(clear)*
He ....

6 All the performances were good, but I was impressed by Jane even more than the others. *(especially)*
All the performances were good, but ....

2 Add the adverb or adjective to each sentence in an appropriate place.

1 The fish smells, I think you should throw it away. *(strange)*
2 You'll have to excuse me, the house is a mess at the moment. *(absolute)*
3 He's able to type with his feet using an adapted keyboard. *(specially)*
4 The database can be transferred to another system with ease. *(relative)*
5 When I got the curtains home, I realised the colour was wrong. *(completely)*
6 The skin around the eyes can be sensitive. *(especially)*
7 The contract states the penalty for late delivery. *(clearly)*
8 Nursery school children will enjoy these experiments with water. *(simple)*
9 He lost in the first round against the tournament's winner. *(eventual)*
10 After hours of discussion, they reached an agreement. *(finally)*

3 Underline the most appropriate words to complete the instructions.

In order to achieve a (1) *strong / strongly* bond, follow the instructions
(2) *careful / carefully*. First ensure that both surfaces are (3) *completely / complete* clean and dry. Spread the adhesive (4) *evenly / even* on both surfaces using the (5) *specially / especially* designed applicator. Allow to dry for a few seconds. (6) *Finally / Eventually*, press the two surfaces together (7) *firm / firmly*. Replace the cap (8) *tight / tightly* after use.

Lie on the floor with your knees bent towards your chest. Clasp your hands (9) *light / lightly* behind your head, keeping your elbows open.

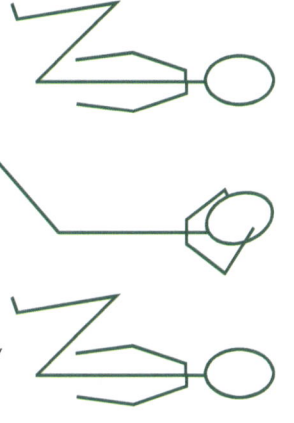

   Breathe in and (10) *slowly / slow* curl your head up from the floor, keeping your chin (11) *slightly / slight* tucked in. As you do so, straighten your legs as much as is (12) *comfortably / comfortable* for you. Make sure you keep your back (13) *flatly / flat* on the floor. Do not push too far, (14) *specially / especially* if you have neck problems.

   Lower your head (15) *gentle / gently* to the floor, bending your knees into your chest. Relax, then repeat the (16) *entire / entirely* exercise again.

  # Chocolate truffles

These rich chocolate truffles are very (17) *simple / simply* to make and are (18) *absolute / absolutely* delicious. Place 340g dark chocolate in a large mixing bowl. Bring 230ml double cream to the boil in a pan and (19) *immediate / immediately* pour it onto the broken chocolate. Mix (20) *thorough / thoroughly* with a wooden spoon until the mixture is (21) *smooth / smoothly* and all the chocolate has melted. Put the mixture in the fridge until it is (22) *complete / completely* cool. Scoop out a teaspoon of the mixture and (23) *gentle / gently* roll it into a ball in the palms of your hands. Roll the truffles in cocoa powder, then (24) *eventually / finally* place them on a tray or plate and put them back in the fridge to set.

28 Commonly confused verbs: *reach / achieve, win / earn, profit / benefit*

1 Tick the correct sentence in each pair.

1   a   *Sadly, he never reached his ambition of playing for his country.*
    b   *Sadly, he never achieved his ambition of playing for his country.*
2   a   *My generation has really benefited from improvements in medicine.*
    b   *My generation has really profited from improvements in medicine.*

We use *reach* followed by a place, or by an age or level:
*We finally **reached the airport** just before 6 o'clock.* (not ~~reached to the airport~~)

We use *achieve* followed by an aim, goal or something you want to do:
*An athlete has to train full time to **achieve success** at the highest level.*

We use *win* to say someone is in the first position in a game, match or competition:
*Who do you think will **win** the World Cup?*

We use *earn* to talk about getting money (from your work):
*Many university lecturers could **earn** more **money** in industry.* (not ~~win more money~~)

We use *profit* (verb and noun) to describe money that someone gets from something, especially an investment or a business:
*A lot of companies will **profit from** the fall in interest rates.*

We use *benefit* to describe other advantages that someone gets from something:
*I speak Italian to my children so that they can **benefit from** learning two languages.*

2 Correct the mistake below.

Nowadays, sports people win more money from sponsorship than from competing.

Nowadays, sports people .... than from competing.

3 Rewrite the sentences below using one of the verbs above.

1   How much are you paid per hour? ....
2   During the day, temperatures can get up to 35°. ....
3   In the 1930s, she was successful as a jazz singer. ....
4   Many old people now live until they're 100. ....
5   A UK company has been awarded the contract. ....
6   Everyone will gain from the opportunities new technology offers. ....
7   He was the last runner to get to the finish line. ....
8   I want to go to university and this scholarship will help me do that. ....

Which verbs are followed by a gerund or an infinitive?

1 Tick the correct sentence in each pair.

1 a Becoming a celebrity often means losing your privacy.
 b Becoming a celebrity often means to lose your privacy.
2 a I couldn't afford buying a new car.
 b I couldn't afford to buy a new car.

Some verbs are followed by a gerund (*-ing*):
- *avoid, enjoy, mean + doing (something)*: He **enjoys playing** golf.

Some verbs are followed by an object + preposition + gerund:
- *accuse (someone) of doing (something)*: She **accused him of having** an affair.
- *criticise (someone) for doing (something)*: The film was **criticised for being** too violent.
- *prevent (someone) from doing (something)*: His injury **prevented him from running**.

The following verbs are followed by an infinitive form (*to do something*):
- *afford, choose, deserve, pretend, strive, struggle + infinitive*:
  He didn't **deserve to lose** his job for such a minor mistake.
- *advise / help / remind (someone) to do (something)*:
  They **advised me to get** travel insurance.

Some verbs can be followed by a gerund or an infinitive, but the meaning changes:
I remember locking the door. (I have a memory of doing it)
I remembered to lock the door. (I didn't forget)

2 Correct the mistake below.

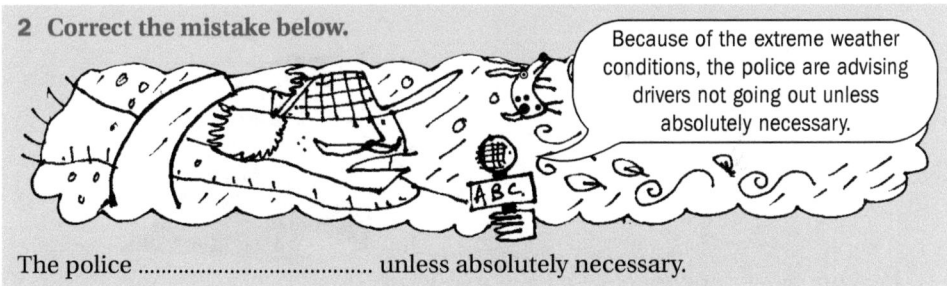

Because of the extreme weather conditions, the police are advising drivers not going out unless absolutely necessary.

The police .... unless absolutely necessary.

3 Complete the sentences using the correct form of the verb in brackets. You may also need to add a preposition in some sentences.

1 I can't imagine .... to a foreign country. *(move)*
2 For some people, 'success' just means .... a lot of money. *(earn)*
3 You should avoid .... dark colours. *(wear)*
4 Have you remembered .... your medicine today? *(take)*
5 I accused him .... the situation. *(exaggerate)*
6 His doctor advised him .... more exercise. *(get)*
7 I was just a young actress struggling .... a living. *(make)*
8 Your PIN code should prevent anyone .... your card. *(use)*

30 Propose, offer or invite?

1 Tick the correct sentence in each pair.

1 a I propose to book a table at the local Italian restaurant.
  b I think we should book a table at the local Italian restaurant.
2 a We offer you a wide range of dishes on our menu.
  b Our menu has a wide range of dishes to choose from.

These verbs are used to describe or report the action of proposing, offering or inviting, but not normally to make a proposal, offer or invitation:
*Steve said '**We could** send clients regular updates via email.'*
*Steve **proposed** (or less formal **suggested**) sending clients regular updates via email.*
☆ *Propose* and *proposal* are quite formal words, mostly used in written business contexts, newspapers, etc. *Suggest* and *suggestion* are less formal alternatives.

*Alison said '**Can I** give you a lift to the station?'*
*I replied 'Thanks for **the offer**, but it'll only take me a few minutes to walk.'*
*Alison **offered to** give me a lift to the station.*
☆ To talk about products, services or facilities we often use *have*, *do* or *provide* instead of *offer* or *propose*:
*Many airlines **do special fares** for students. (not airlines propose)*

*Dave said 'I'm going to the cinema this evening. **Would you like to come?**'*
*Dave **invited me (to go) to the cinema** with him.*
*Mark and Sharon have sent me **an invitation to their wedding**.*

2 Correct the mistake below.

Government announces .... to 16.

3 Complete the sentences with appropriate written or spoken language.

1 Tom suggested that we hitchhike. – 'Why .... ?'
2 Janice .... while we're away. – 'I'll look after the garden.'
3 Children's special: half-size portions. – 'We .... for children.'
4 Alex .... tomorrow. – 'We could visit the site tomorrow.'
5 The waiter .... – 'Can I take your coat for you?'
6 Kerry invited us to dinner. – 'Would .... for dinner?'
7 Steve's suggestion was for a barbecue. – 'I think we ....'
8 I asked about conference facilities. – 'Do .... conference facilities?'

TEST 10

1 Complete the text using one of the verbs from the box in an appropriate form. Some verbs are not used.

struggle	benefit	achieve	accuse	criticise	profit
reach	prevent	enjoy	avoid	mean	advise

A number of recent surveys have shown that obesity amongst children in Britain has (1) .... alarming levels. Some experts have (2) .... food companies for actively promoting junk food to children They (3) .... them of aiming much of their advertising at the children themselves, which makes life even more difficult for parents who are (4) .... to encourage healthy eating habits. So how can you (5) .... your child from becoming overweight? Nutritionists (6) .... parents to find healthy alternatives to sugary snacks, such as fruit or nuts, and to (7) .... giving children too many processed foods at mealtimes. Children can also (8) .... from plenty of physical activity. This doesn't have to be organised sports – most children (9) .... running around, so make the most of any opportunity for them to go out and play in the garden or at the park. This might (10) .... washing a few more muddy clothes, but surely that's a small price to pay for your child's health!

2 In each of the following sentences there is a preposition missing. Add an appropriate preposition in the correct place.

1 Have you had an invitation Helen's party? ....
2 His doctor advised him rest for a few days. ....
3 Maintenance staff were criticised not reporting the problem earlier. ....
4 Police prevented protesters entering the parliament building. ....
5 Working mothers stand to benefit most more flexible working hours. ....
6 Are you accusing me cheating? ....
7 She gave a talk about the benefits yoga and meditation. ....
8 Who will profit the sale of these buildings? ....

3 Complete the sentences below using the correct form of the verbs in the box.

offer	propose	suggest	provide	hire	book	investigate	mean

Nicki: Why don't we have a barbecue in the college grounds?
Lucy: I can help arrange the cooking if you like.
Ben: Yes, but what if it rains? It might (1) .... cancelling the whole thing.

Nicky:	We could always get a marquee so people have somewhere dry to go.
Andy:	I'll have to check whether we can afford (2) .... something big enough.
Simon:	It'd be great to get a local band to come and play too.
Ben:	Yeah, that's a good idea. I'll look into it.

Student Entertainment Committee Minutes

At Thursday's meeting of the Student Entertainment Committee a number of suggestions were put forward for the end-of-term party. Nicki (3) .... having a barbecue and Lucy (4) .... to arrange the catering. Ben raised the issue of the weather and Nicki (5) .... that we hire a marquee to (6) .... cover in case of rain. Andy will check the budget regarding this proposal. Simon proposed (7) .... a local band to play and Ben offered (8) .... the possibility.

4 Match the two parts of the sentences below.

1 Many illegal workers earn ....   a sitting out in the sun at midday.
2 A friend of mine won ....   b your skin from getting burnt.
3 Our campaign has achieved ....   c less than $2 an hour.
4 You should avoid ....   d dangerously high levels.
5 Always wear sunblock to prevent ....   e special last-minute offers.
6 Pollution in the city has reached ....   f £10,000 on the lottery.
7 Lots of travel agents do ....   g some useful sightseeing suggestions.
8 Our tour representative made ....   h its objectives.

5 Complete the second sentence using the word in brackets so that it sounds more natural in spoken English.

1 Kate proposed that we could get Tim a stereo for his birthday. *(suggest)*
   Kate .... for his birthday.
2 Can I offer you a drink? *(like)*
   Would .... a drink?
3 The ring was offered to me by my mother when I was 13. *(give)*
   My mother .... when I was 13.
4 Many restaurants provide vegetarian meals. *(do)*
   Lots of .... vegetarian meals.
5 Jack put forward a proposal that we swap rooms. *(suggest)*
   Jack .... rooms.
6 Matthew invited me to have dinner with him. *(ask)*
   Matthew ....

Answer key

Unit 1
1 1 b
2 a
2 told me last week that you would come and fix
3 1 would be
2 would call
3 continues
4 will double
5 would be
6 goes
7 would be
8 were

Unit 2
1 1 a
2 a
2 must not be left
3 1 must
2 don't have to
3 had to
4 can't
5 must
6 must
7 should
8 mustn't / shouldn't

Unit 3
1 1 a
2 a
2 looking after my baby brother to listen to my problems
3 1 He has / had a terrible fear of travelling by plane.
2 She was right to tell her boss about the problem.
3 He has / had the ability to play at the highest level of the sport.
4 We had difficulty finding a parking space.
5 It isn't / wasn't worth cooking a full meal for one person.
6 I feel lucky to have such good friends.
7 He didn't have the courage to tell her face to face.

8 He isn't / wasn't used to getting up so early.

Test 1
1 1 should
2 have to
3 should
4 have to
5 should
6 shouldn't
7 should
8 have to
9 should
2 1 would stop smoking
2 she would call (me) when she arrived
3 I would have
4 would be finished / would have been finished
5 would bring
6 would be living
7 would take
3 1 to push
2 will bring
3 should
4 to go
5 have to
6 worrying
7 should
8 have to
9 will be
4 1 to get / to receive
2 having
3 can't be / isn't
4 to ban / to punish
5 of taking
6 to punish / to penalise
7 to enforce
8 to lose
9 paying
5 workers **have to** work; for fear **of losing**; have difficulty **earning**; are happy **to accept**; **has to** travel; **should** do something.

Unit 4
1 1 a
2 b
2 which has a warm, dry climate

3 1 There are many students who can't afford to pay such high fees.

2 … in a / this country which has free basic healthcare.

3 … two main characters who are very different.

4 He hasn't explained what he wants me to do.

5 … with a lovely family who live in an old farmhouse.

6 People are living longer, which means that …

7 Do you know what he plans to do …

8 My uncle, who is a bank manager, gave me some helpful advice …

Unit 5

1 1 a

2 b

2 what if they're wrong?

3 1 yourself

2 their

3 you

4 your

5 you

6 they

7 you

8 their

Unit 6

1 1 b

2 b

2 get themselves into trouble

3 1 themselves

2 ourselves

3 yourself

4 themselves

5 us

6 yourselves

7 yourself

8 themselves

Test 2

1 1 who

2 which

3 which

4 who

5 what

6 who

7 which

8 what

2 1 Everyone should play their part in helping protect the environment.

2 Tourists should respect the local customs of the country they are visiting.

3 If you promise to do something, you shouldn't go back on your promise.

4 When someone enters a mosque, they are expected to remove their shoes.

5 If a person is found guilty of a crime, they have to accept the punishment.

3 1 who

2 you

3 you

4 they

5 you

6 you

7 who

8 themselves

9 which

10 who

11 what

12 ourselves

4 charity **which** helps; people **who** are homeless; over **their heads**; **They** may require; programmes **which** help; develop **their** self-confidence; support **they need**; rebuild **their lives**

5 1 found themselves

2 be yourself

3 express themselves

4 enjoy ourselves

5 lock themselves out

6 take care of ourselves

7 please yourselves

Unit 7

1 1 b

2 b

2 we didn't live on the top floor

3 1 in the future

2 *correct*

3 at the age of

4 the world is

5   in the next village
6   the worst accident
7   *correct*
8   The weather got worse

Unit 8
1 1 a
    2 a
2 it was quite a tough race
3 1 I went to quite a large school.
    2 We had a really wonderful holiday. / We really had …
    3 My family are very important to me.
    4 Maybe his story really was true.
    5 The software is quite easy to use.
    6 Everyone worked really hard to finish on time.
    7 We live fairly close to the city centre.
    8 Their apartment is in quite a new building.

Unit 9
1 1 b
    2 a
2 far fewer tourists visited the region last year
3 1 fewer
    2 less
    3 fewer
    4 the least
    5 less
    6 Fewer
    7 less
    8 less

Test 3
1 1 a
    2 —
    3 the
    4 —
    5 the
    6 —
    7 The
    8 a
    9 the
    10 —
2 1 … at the age of 60. / at age 60.
    2 are fewer independent record labels than

3   in quite a rich sauce
4   got / had the impression (that) she didn't want
5   the college really is likely
6   spend less time with my family than
7   was the only foreigner
8   to change our staffing levels in the short term
9   on Friday evening and was taken to hospital the next day.
10   the least expensive dish on the menu
3 1 really / very
    2 fewer
    3 more
    4 very / really
    5 quite
    6 slightly
    7 less
4 1 fewer
    2 the largest / biggest
    3 less
    4 few
    5 the main
    6 Fewer
5 contains **the** minimum doses; suffer from **fewer** minor illnesses; are also **less** likely; contain **very** high concentrations; the **really** important thing; of **the** whole fruit; in **the** form of

Unit 10
1 1 b
    2 a
2 a rapid increase in mobile phone ownership
3 1 in
    2 of
    3 in
    4 from
    5 to
    6 in
    7 of
    8 in
    9 of
    10 of
    11 in

Unit 11

1 1 b
  2 a
2 depends on the weather really
3 1 concentrate on
  2 insist on
  3 consists of
  4 depend on
  5 contribute to
  6 concentrate more on
  7 insisted on
  8 depends on

Unit 12

1 1 a
  2 a
2 at the moment. Can I call you back later?
3 1 At the end
  2 at the time
  3 At that time
  4 by the time
  5 *correct*
  6 at that moment
  7 *correct*
  8 By midday

Test 4

1 1 of
  2 in
  3 of
  4 to
  5 on
  6 in / of
  7 in
  8 from / by
  9 to
  10 in
  11 of
  12 of
2 1 revealed a drop in profits of
    £1million
  2 aims to stop the spread of AIDS
  3 that there has been a rise in
    temperatures of 1.5°
  4 rapid growth in the number of
    people using
  5 unhappy about the decline in
  6 can lead to weight gain in

  7 is aiming for a reduction of 25% in
  8 there has been a decrease of 12% in
3 1 At
  2 at
  3 by
  4 at
4 1 drop
  2 moment
  3 fall
  4 concentrate
  5 time
  6 growth
5 1 at
  2 by
  3 at
  4 by
  5 by
  6 by
  7 by
  8 at
  9 by
  10 at

Unit 13

1 1 a
  2 b
2 not discuss my religious beliefs
3 1 people
  2 life
  3 children
  4 beliefs
  5 aircraft
  6 lives, people / children
  7 belief
  8 families

Unit 14

1 1 b
  2 a
2 something you don't see every day
3 1 every day
  2 every time
  3 every day
  4 everybody
  5 every one
  6 everyone
  7 everyday

8 everything

Unit 15
1 1 b
  2 b
2 Passengers travelling from
3 1 labelled
  2 equalled
  3 got
  4 metres
  5 organizations
  6 learned, traveling
  7 recognize
  8 spelled

Test 5
1 1 Everyday, before
  2 people, persons, official / formal
  3 –ies, storey
  4 got, gotten
  5 -l, one consonant / l
2 1 aeroplane
  2 canceled
  3 traveling
  4 spelt / spelled
  5 realize
  6 gotten
  7 colour
  8 signaled
3 the **everyday lives**; the **people** living
there; many **families**; tin **rooves**;
everyone was really friendly; especially
the **children**; I **travelled** on;
3,350 **metres**; Lots of **travellers**; they've
got used to; amazing **stories**
4 1 wife
  2 wives
  3 aircraft
  4 aircraft
  5 signal
  6 signalled
  7 signaled
  8 counsellor
  9 counselor
5 1 lives
  2 people
  3 counsellors
  4 cancelled

5 aircraft
6 Travellers

Unit 16
1 1 b
  2 b
2 stand up for yourself
3 1 in for
  2 up for / (stood) by
  3 up for
  4 up
  5 up for / (stood) by
  6 by
  7 in for
  8 by

Unit 17
1 1 a
  2 b
2 capable of taking care of myself
3 1 took part in
  2 *correct*
  3 took a step back
  4 to take part in
  5 will take place in
  6 to take care of himself
  7 *correct*
  8 take good care of it

Unit 18
1 1 a
  2 b
2 You look lost
3 1 risen
  2 lose
  3 losing
  4 rose
  5 lost
  6 losses (a loss)
  7 loss
  8 raised

Test 6
1 1 have risen by 5%
  2 need to be taken into account
  3 will take care of you
  4 do not want to raise their children
  5 cause loss of appetite
  6 getting out of bed

7 will take place in Brighton

8 stands in for a stage actor

2 1 part

2 place

3 lost

4 raised

5 take

6 lost

7 raised

8 standing

3 1 will take place / takes place in Bristol

2 raise money

3 wants to take part in the run should / can get an application form

4 will have the chance / will be able to raise

5 will be taken into consideration

6 will take place / takes place

7 against job losses

8 standing up for

4 1 up

2 of

3 after

4 in

5 of

6 for

7 into

8 in

5 1 d

2 e

3 f

4 b

5 c

6 h

7 a

8 g

Unit 19

1 1 b

2 a

2 is the best way to study / way of studying

3 1 route

2 methods

3 way

4 means

5 method

6 way

7 routes

8 means

Unit 20

1 1 a

2 a

2 a more interesting job

3 1 careers

2 work

3 job

4 work

5 career (or job)

6 jobs

7 work

8 work

Unit 21

1 1 b

2 a

2 trade relations between our two nations

3 1 relationship

2 relations / relatives

3 relations

4 relationship

5 relationship

6 upbringing

7 Relations

8 education

Test 7

1 1 work

2 means

3 route

4 journey

5 way

6 job

7 ways

8 method

2 1 relations

2 work

3 way

4 job

5 method

6 relationship

7 path

8 relatives, relative

3
1. my upbringing
2. close relationship with
3. at work
4. *correct*
5. way to pay (method of payment / of paying *are acceptable in written English*)
6. in relations between
7. out of work / out of a job
8. *correct*

4
1. relative / relation
2. upbringings
3. job / education
4. career
5. paths
6. relationship
7. career
8. work
9. work
10. career
11. path (route is also acceptable)
12. job
13. routes
14. means
15. routes
16. work

Unit 22
1 1 b
    2 b

2 really affected the tourist industry / trade *(tourism is also acceptable)*

3
1. destinations
2. tourism
3. economic
4. tourist attractions
5. holiday
6. economy
7. economical
8. The growth of tourism

Unit 23
1 1 a
    2 a

2 by a mutual friend

3
1. shared
2. common
3. usual
4. average / ordinary
5. common (usual *is also acceptable*)
6. mutual
7. ordinary
8. common

Unit 24
1 1 a
    2 a

2 is essential / absolutely essential / very important

3
1. vital
2. important
3. significant
4. relevant
5. important
6. important
7. fundamental
8. relevant

Test 8
1
1. f
2. c
3. h
4. g
5. a
6. d
7. b
8. e

2 the most **common** cause; A **significant** minority; a **fundamental** reason; for schools **to alter** their approach; more **relevant to**; **ordinary** young people; It is vital that; will be important to them; the **average** teenager; a **significant** increase

3
1. average
2. significant
3. fundamental
4. The usual procedure
5. essential
6. common
7. a joint decision
8. relevant to

4 Across
1. holiday resort
4. looser
6. fun

7 crucial
11 again
12 trade
13 essential
Down
2 destination
3 touristy
5 relevant
6 fundamental
8 usual
9 ordinary
10 average

Unit 25
1 1 b
  2 a
2 explain that again more simply
3 1 gently
  2 heavily
  3 completely
  4 thick
  5 warm
  6 quiet
  7 busiest
  8 complete

Unit 26
1 1 b
  2 a
2 I especially enjoy baking / I enjoy baking, especially
3 1 especially if it's raining
  2 *correct*
  3 Women especially should be careful (women need to be more careful than men) / Women should be especially careful (they should be very careful)
  4 especially in
  5 which is specially designed
  6 *correct*
  7 The museum is especially renowned
  8 is it especially cold

Unit 27
1 1 a
  2 b
2 finally, he told me / he finally told me that I'd passed

3 1 eventually
  2 possible
  3 actually
  4 Finally
  5 eventually
  6 eventual
  7 eventually / finally
  8 finally

Test 9
1 1 his story was completely true
  2 finally got to the hotel
  3 take part in the race in specially-made
  4 stood there in absolute silence
  5 gave us clear instructions
  6 I was especially impressed by Jane
2 1 The fish smells strange
  2 the house is an absolute mess
  3 a specially-adapted keyboard
  4 with relative ease
  5 the colour was completely wrong
  6 can be especially sensitive
  7 contract clearly states / states clearly the penalty
  8 these simple experiments
  9 the tournament's eventual winner
  10 they finally reached / finally they reached / Finally, after hours
3 1 strong
  2 carefully
  3 completely
  4 evenly
  5 specially
  6 Finally
  7 firmly
  8 tightly
  9 lightly
  10 slowly
  11 slightly
  12 comfortable
  13 flat
  14 especially
  15 gently
  16 entire
  17 simple
  18 absolutely

19 immediately
20 thoroughly
21 smooth
22 completely
23 gently
24 finally

Unit 28
1 1 b
   2 a
2 earn more money from sponsorship
3 1 do you earn per hour
   2 can reach 35°
   3 she achieved success as
   4 now reach the age of
   5 has won the contract
   6 will benefit from
   7 to reach the finishing line
   8 will help me achieve that

Unit 29
1 1 a
   2 b
2 are advising drivers not to go out
3 1 moving
   2 earning
   3 wearing
   4 to take
   5 of exaggerating
   6 to get
   7 to make
   8 from using

Unit 30
1 1 b
   2 b
2 proposal to cut the voting age
3 1 don't we hitchhike
   2 offered to look after the garden
   3 do / have half-size portions
   4 proposed visiting the site /
      suggested (that) we visit the site
   5 offered to take my coat
   6 you like to come (over / round)
   7 should have a barbecue
   8 you have / provide

Test 10
1 1 reached
   2 criticised
   3 accuse / accused
   4 struggling
   5 prevent
   6 advise
   7 avoid
   8 benefit
   9 enjoy
  10 mean
2 1 invitation to
   2 advised him to
   3 criticised for
   4 prevented protesters from
   5 benefit most from
   6 accusing me of
   7 the benefits of
   8 profit from
3 1 mean
   2 to hire
   3 proposed / suggested
   4 offered
   5 suggested / proposed
   6 provide
   7 booking
   8 to investigate
4 1 c
   2 f
   3 h
   4 a
   5 b
   6 d
   7 e
   8 g
5 1 suggested (that) we (could) get Tim
      a stereo / suggested getting Tim a
      stereo
   2 you like
   3 gave me the ring
   4 restaurants do
   5 suggested (that) we swap /
      suggested swapping
   6 asked me to have dinner with him /
      asked me out to dinner

Acknowledgements

The author would like to thank Helen Forrest for her help and input in editing the manuscript, and all her friends in Geneva for their inspiration and encouragement in the writing of this book.

Illustrated by Julian Mosedale

The Cambridge Learner Corpus
This book is based on information from the Cambridge Learner Corpus, a collection of over 50,000 exam papers from Cambridge ESOL. It shows real mistakes students make, and highlights which parts of English cause particular problems for learners.

The Cambridge Learner Corpus has been developed jointly with the University of Cambridge ESOL Examinations and forms part of the Cambridge International Corpus.

To find out more, visit
www.cambridge.org/elt/corpus